BEAR GRYLLS

SURVIVAL CAMP

BEAR GRYLLS

SURVIVAL CAMP

THE ULTIMATE ALL-TERRAIN TRAINING

CONTENTS

Oceans & Rivers

Navigation

SURVIVAL CAMP

INTRODUCTION

I've been so lucky in my life to have been on some truly incredible adventures around the world. From the icy cold of the Arctic to the scorching heat of the desert, from the thin air and icy faces of Everest to the humid, snake and mosquito-filled jungles of the Tropics. I've battled the elements and survived the extremes and through it all I have learned two things.

Firstly, that the human spirit is incredible and we are all capable of much more than we might think. Our persistence, courage, positivity, and determination are always our greatest weapon.

Secondly, I have learned that knowledge is power. If you want to survive efficiently then you have to learn as much as you can about the techniques and the skills needed for the wild.

So whether you find yourself lost in a jungle, dehydrated in a desert, facing off with a bear in a forest, or lost at sea, this book is here to help empower you with the skills and knowledge to survive. I have packed this book full of tips and tricks I have learned to help you survive almost any extreme situation.

Our planet is an incredible place and life is all about adventure, so get out there and explore!

Bear.

ESSENTIAL GEAR

Packing for an explorer's adventure isn't like packing for a trip to the beach, although in both cases you should take a hat. Unless you are the Duke of Abruzzi, grandson of the king of Italy, who traveled to Alaska in 1897 with dozens of servants and porters, and four cast-iron beds, you will probably have to plan carefully so that you can carry all the gear you need in a single backpack.

Boot up

Unless you are planning to fly or sail for the entire expedition, you will need to rely on your own two feet at some point, making the right boots possibly your most important piece of equipment. Your boots need to be a perfect mixture: light and flexible but sturdy and waterproof, warm but not too sweaty. The exact boot will depend on where you are going.

Basic hiking boot

- For walking and exploring in forest, mountains, rough ground, or grassland anywhere in the temperate zone (places that are not too hot and not too cold), this boot is best.

- It is tough but flexible and relatively lightweight, and will let your foot breathe.

Jungle boot

- Made from canvas and rubber to cope with wet ground and constant rainfall, waterproof below and quick-drying above.

- This boot is tough enough to resist thorns, insect bites, and snake fangs, but light enough not to overheat your feet.

Mountain boot

- Much more rigid than hiking boots, these boots are stiff and heavy but keep your feet warm and dry in snow and ice, and won't slip or buckle when jammed against a rock.

Desert boot

- Usually made of suede, which keeps out hot sand, but is very light and lets your feet breathe to stay relatively cool.

Bear necessities

Pack a few warm but light and quick-drying clothes, a sleeping bag suited to your destination (don't take a heavy, super warm one to a jungle), waterproof jacket, fire-lighting equipment, first-aid kit, maps and compass, and survival gear. This should be in a tough container like a tin, and should be kept on you at all times. It should have: a button compass, fishing line and hook, lighter, wire saw, and a needle and thread.

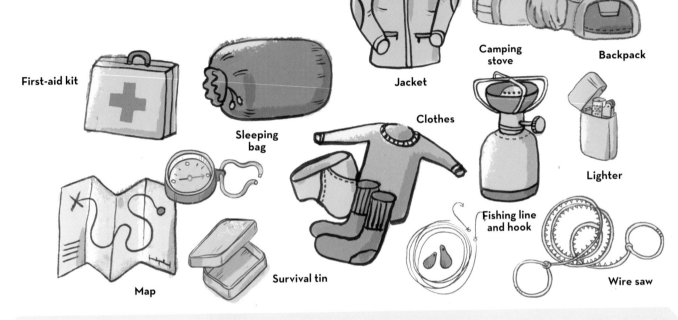

First-aid kit

Jacket

Camping stove

Backpack

Sleeping bag

Clothes

Lighter

Map

Survival tin

Fishing line and hook

Wire saw

DOUBLE UP

The best gear is stuff that is multiuse. For instance, when Norwegian polar explorer Fridtjof Nansen made the first crossing of Greenland in 1888, he used the groundsheet from his tent as both a sail for his sled and the bottom of a makeshift boat.

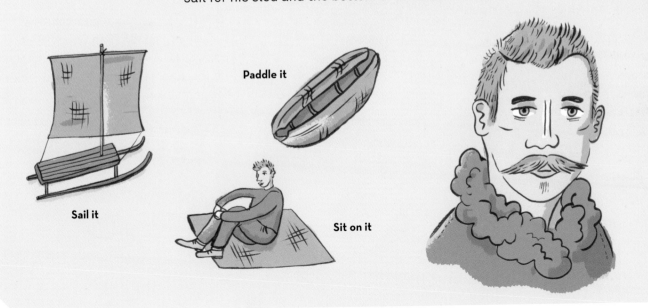

Paddle it

Sail it

Sit on it

JUNGLE & SAVANNAH

You're hacking your way through the jungle with your machete, when suddenly the ground gives way and you slide down a muddy ravine, tumbling through a giant spider's web and into a pool of deadly quicksand. The crumbling ruins of an ancient temple loom on either side. Should you call for help or grab a vine and haul yourself out?

EXPLORER'S QUEST

The tropical regions of the world, with their thick jungles and wide, grassy savannahs, are rich in exotic animals and unsolved mysteries – in other words, they are perfect for explorers. Will you track down the lost treasure city of the Inca or find the source of the Nile?

Finding the source

Victorian explorers were obsessed with tracing the course of the world's longest river – the Nile – and discovering its source deep in the African interior. Can you retrace their footsteps and make the journey across the "Mountains of the Moon"?

Monster snakes

The biggest snakes in the world are found in the rain forests of South America, Africa and Indonesia; some are over 33 feet long. But there have been rumors of much bigger snakes, so enormous that they could swallow whole canoes. Can these legendary snakes really exist, and can you stun the world of science by finding one?

BEAR SAYS

We have everything to learn from traditional tribes: tracking, hunting, and survival skills. But we must be careful not to pass on to them our own diseases and bad habits!

Welcome to the world

Thousands of tribes make the thick jungles of the world their home. Some tribes are so remote that they have never been contacted by the modern world. Can you be the first to introduce yourself to an uncontacted tribe?

BIG GAME

For the big-game hunters who visited Africa looking for animal heads to stick on their walls, nothing compared to the "Big Five" – the animals considered most dangerous and difficult to hunt: lion, elephant, leopard, rhinoceros, and buffalo. Can you track down these fierce beasts and shoot them in a less bloodthirsty way – with your camera?

Lion  **Elephant**  **Leopard**  **Rhinoceros**  **Buffalo**

Lost city of the Inca

In the early 1500s, the Spanish conquistador Francisco Pizarro conquered the Inca empire, but some Inca escaped over the mountains into the Amazon rain forest, taking with them a vast fortune in gold. Adventurers and explorers have long believed that they founded a secret city in the jungle, which might yet contain a fabulous treasure beyond belief. Could you be the one to discover the lost city when so many others have died trying?

BEAR SAYS

Before setting out, plan your expedition: what gear, maps, and training do you need?

IT'S A JUNGLE OUT THERE

Emergent layer

Canopy layer

Jungle terrain is difficult to move through, and the combination of heat and constant rain makes it very uncomfortable – as do the swarms of insects.

Jungle anatomy

This illustration shows how the jungle is divided into vertical levels, with giant trees forming a thick canopy that blocks out most of the light. Down at ground level, the plants are crowded together, making it hard to move around. Your machete is the most important piece of gear you have! (But always use it with adult supervision.)

Understory layer

BEAR SAYS

There's plenty of rain in the rain forest, but little fresh drinking water. Learn to recognize water vines – they hold fresh water in their hollow stems. Use your machete to hack them open.

Shrub layer

Herb layer

14

JUNGLE GEAR

You need clothes and gear that will cope with heat, constant rain, and insects. Clothes need to be light and loose to keep you cool, tough so that they don't get shredded by thorns and spikes, and quick drying so that you're not constantly damp.

Whetstone for sharpening your machete

Insect repellent

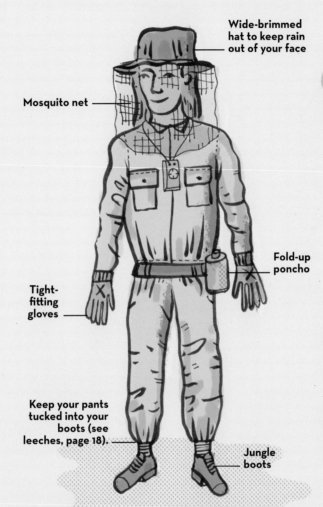

Wide-brimmed hat to keep rain out of your face

Mosquito net

Tight-fitting gloves

Fold-up poncho

Keep your pants tucked into your boots (see leeches, page 18).

Jungle boots

Plastic map case

Waterproof bags

HOW TO USE A MACHETE

A machete is a long-bladed knife for slashing a path through leaves and vines. Get your technique right or you will waste precious energy and take too long to get through the jungle. Always cut at an angle, and keep your wrist parallel to the cut. Chop down to cut through stems and vines, and up to cut through leaves. Follow a three-step cut:

1 Let your shoulder drop.

2 Lead with your elbow.

3 Flick your wrist at the last second.

RIVER MONSTERS

The best way to get around in the jungle is to travel by river, but you won't be the only one in the water! Crocodiles and alligators infest the waterways of the tropical world, and they're not even the worst things.

Piranha safety

Rivers in the Amazon are infested with deadly piranhas – small fish with razor-sharp teeth. They attack in shoals of 20 or more, and can strip all the flesh off an animal in minutes, leaving just bones. Here's how to swim with piranhas and survive:

1 Swim at night – piranhas are active during the day.

2 Avoid low rivers and pools left behind during the dry season – piranhas attack in large numbers only when they are hungry and desperate. In the wet season, a river at its normal level should be safe, but in the dry season, when water and food levels are low, piranhas become more dangerous.

3 Chuck in some meat – throw an animal carcass into the river downstream and cross while the piranhas are busy eating it.

HOW TO WRESTLE A CROCODILE

Crocodiles and alligators were swimming in rivers when dinosaurs walked the Earth. Their mouths are packed with teeth and they're horribly strong, but they do have weaknesses. If you're attacked by an alligator or a (smallish) crocodile you can fight back!

1 Distract the croc. You need to get on the croc's back, but you could end up jumping in its mouth if it's not distracted – get someone else to wave and shout at it. If you're on your own, throw your T-shirt over its eyes.

2 Jump on its back. Aim for its neck, just in front of its front legs. When you land on it, push its head down – it can't do much while its head is on the ground.

River crossings

If you're trekking in the jungle, sooner or later you'll have to cross a river. The best way is to fix a rope line and climb over the water, but someone has to go over first to set it up.

Float aids

You can quickly make a flotation aid by tying the legs of your pants into knots at the ankles. Swing the pants through the air to fill them up, like a balloon, then thrust them into the water.

Rope or nail some logs together

You can whip up a quick raft by lashing a few short logs together with rope.

Make a raft

To cross a really big river it might be worth taking a day or two to build a proper raft.

The only tools you'll need

3 Lift up its back legs. Use your back legs to pin the croc's back legs to its sides while keeping its feet off the ground. This will stop it from rolling over on you.

4 Blind the croc. Slide one hand down the middle of its head until you're covering the eyes; it will pull them back into its head. Press down.

5 Hold its mouth closed. Slide one hand around its bottom jaw line and clamp its mouth shut. Now bring your other hand down to hold the other side shut.

6 Pull its head back. Pull the head up and towards you. When the croc's head is pointing up, it is at your mercy.

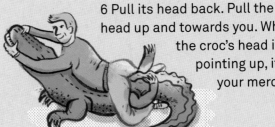

SUCKERS AND STINGERS

The jungle might be full of adventure and mystery, but unfortunately it's also full of horrible things that want to bite, sting, and eat you.

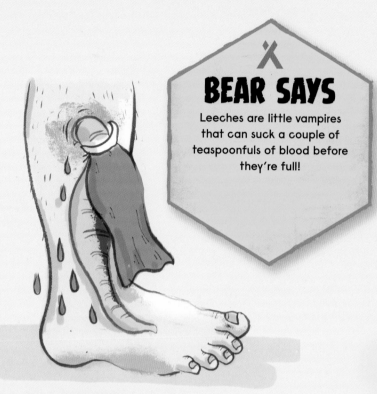

BEAR SAYS

Leeches are little vampires that can suck a couple of teaspoonfuls of blood before they're full!

Leeches

In the jungle, leeches are everywhere. They can smell you – stand still long enough and you'll see some dropping off leaves and squirming towards you. Leeches attach to any exposed skin and suck your blood. You have to be careful about removing them so the bites don't collect germs.

TO REMOVE A LEECH...

1 Look for the small end – this is its head. Use your fingernail to loosen it, then flick it away.

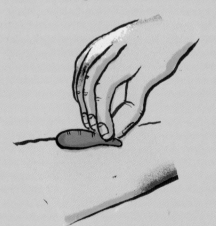

2 You can force a leech to let go with salt, alcohol, vinegar, or a flame, but this might make it vomit blood and germs into the bite wound. It's probably better to keep flicking or wait until the leech is full, when it will drop off.

3 Immediately clean the wound with antiseptic – in the jungle even tiny bites can quickly become nasty infections.

Creepy crawlies

The jungle is home to the greatest variety of insects anywhere on the planet. A lot of these insects see you as a meal, a home, or target practice. This is especially bad news in the jungle because every bite, wound, or scratch is a horrible infection waiting to happen. Check yourself frequently, keep any bites clean and covered, and treat them with disinfectant.

Ticks
These nasty little bloodsuckers clamp onto you. Some carry deadly diseases, but don't try to rip them out in case their head parts break off in your skin. Choke them with tree sap or oil.

Bees
In the jungle, bees are bigger and nastier than the ones you are used to. If you disturb a hive or swarm, try not to panic. Protect your eyes and mouth and walk quickly away, through a bush if possible. If you have a clear path you might even outrun them. If you get stung, take out the bee stingers carefully with a blunt knife edge or fingernail.

STINGING TREES

As if the animals weren't bad enough, in the jungle even the trees are vicious. Stinging trees are covered in tiny "hairs," like minute shards of glass, which are full of poison. They are so fine that they get into your skin, even through clothing, and can drive you mad with pain. If you can't avoid them, you can get them out using hair-removal wax or adhesive tape.

Botflies
Botfly babies bore into your skin and wriggle about in your flesh. Learn how to remove them on page 23.

Poisonous caterpillars
Hairy, brightly colored caterpillars may be dangerous. If one lands on you, brush it off with your machete blade, brushing in the direction of its head.

LOST CITIES OF GOLD

Explorers dream of filling in the great blank spaces on the map, and two of the biggest and blankest spaces in western history were the great jungles of Africa and South America. Add the possibility of finding vast treasure, and it's easy to see why.

El Dorado

Early European explorers in South America dreamed of discovering the legendary El Dorado (Spanish for "the Golden One"), a city of gold hidden in the Amazon jungle. Hundreds of men died trying to find this place, which probably never existed. The famous English explorer Sir Walter Raleigh tried to find El Dorado in what is now Guyana and Venezuela in 1617, but his trip was not a great success. His son was killed, his best friend shot himself when things went wrong, and his head was cut off when he got home.

BEAR SAYS

Raleigh's mistake was that he lost his head – literally! In the wild, it is essential to stay level-headed. Accidents happen when you start to panic, or set yourself unrealistic goals.

Dr. Livingstone, I presume

David Livingstone was a Scottish doctor and missionary who crossed the Kalahari Desert and explored central Africa, where he spread Christianity and fought the slave trade. Then he went missing on an expedition to find the source of the Nile, deep in the jungle. In 1871 the English-American journalist and adventurer Henry Morton Stanley was sent to find him. After seven months, Stanley found Livingstone on the shores of Lake Tanganyika. The Scottish explorer was probably the only other white man for a thousand miles, but Stanley famously greeted him with the polite question, "Dr. Livingstone, I presume?" Livingstone later died while still hunting the source of the Nile, and Stanley went on to explore the Congo, the greatest jungle river in Africa.

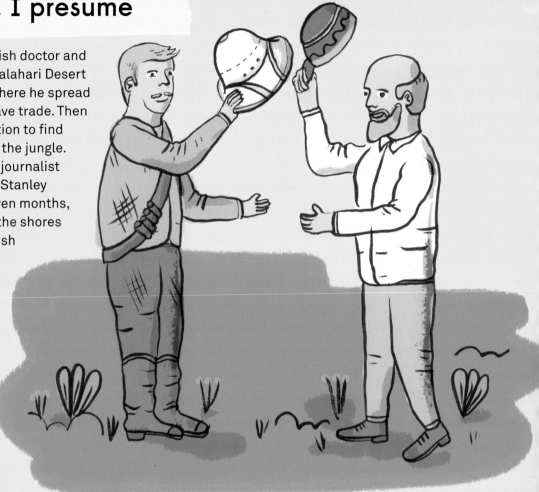

The lost city of Z

Another man who believed in a mysterious city of gold in the Amazon was the British explorer Colonel Percy Fawcett. He called the lost city "Z," and believed it was a place of magical power. He had many adventures in the deep jungle, during which he claimed to have shot a 65-foot-long anaconda and discovered a two-nosed dog. In 1925, Fawcett disappeared while exploring the dangerous Matto Grosso region of the Amazon rain forest. Nearly 50 explorers have died while searching for some trace of Fawcett, but his body has never been discovered.

JUNGLE SURVIVORS

The jungle is dangerous and difficult, but it can also provide everything you need to stay alive, if you know how to find it. The stories of the Gremlin Special crash and Juliane Koepcke offer valuable survival tips for jungle explorers.

BEAR SAYS

You can't survive in the jungle without listening to the advice of local people. They know which plants are safe to eat, where to find water, and how to keep clear of predators.

Cannibal crash landing

During World War II, United States Air Force pilots discovered a hidden jungle valley in the center of New Guinea. The people who lived there had never made contact with the outside world. It was impossible for airplanes to land there and the overland route was blocked by Japanese soldiers and native headhunters. This didn't stop military people from flying over the valley for thrill rides, and in 1945 an airplane called the Gremlin Special crashed into a mountainside. Twenty-one people died, but three people survived. Thanks to the help of local tribespeople, they survived until a daring rescue was arranged, involving a glider and an airplane with a big hook.

The woman who fell out of a plane

Seventeen-year-old Juliane Koepcke was flying over the Amazon jungle in 1971 when her plane was hit by lightning and broke into pieces in midair. Amazingly, she survived falling from 2 miles up, crashing through the trees and landing with little more than a black eye. Everyone else on the plane, including her mother, was killed. Lost in the middle of thick jungle and with nothing to eat except a few pieces of candy, Koepcke remembered some advice from her father: find a stream and follow it downhill. Streams lead to rivers, and rivers will eventually lead to people. Koepcke walked for days along a stream until she found an empty cabin. By now her skin was infested with baby botflies, so to get rid of them she poured gasoline over her wounds and pulled out 50 larvae. Soon after, some lumberjacks turned up and she was rescued.

REMOVING A BOTFLY LARVA

1 The larva needs to breathe. Suffocate it with duct tape or petroleum jelly.

2 Apply pressure around the wound, then pinch the larva tail when it emerges.

3 Pull steadily until the larva is completely out. Clean and bandage the wound.

ESCAPING QUICKSAND

Quicksand is a mixture of fine sand, clay, and water. In the movies when someone steps in quicksand they get sucked in, and the more they struggle the more they sink, until they drown. Thankfully, in real life you won't sink deeper than your chest. But quicksand is very hard to get out of, so you could die if you are stuck too long!

BEAR SAYS

As with all dangers, the best way to save yourself is prevention. Watch out for quicksand around lakes, on riverbanks, near the coast, and in marshes. Test the ground with a stick.

Sticky situation

Quicksand is strange stuff: it can change from being as solid as concrete to being oozy like porridge, depending on whether it is being stirred around. When you tread on quicksand, you start mixing it up, so it goes porridgy and you start to sink in. But it is impossible for a person to completely sink into quicksand because the human body is less dense than quicksand, so you will always end up floating in it – probably no deeper than your waist. Quicksand can kill you in other ways, though! Once you stop moving, the quicksand sets into its hard form, and it becomes incredibly hard to pull yourself out. This means you could easily get stuck until you starve, or until you're drowned in a flood.

Swimming in porridge

To get out of quicksand, you first need to stop yourself from sinking in too deep.

1 As soon as you realize you are in trouble, take off your pack and throw it to one side.

2 Lie down on your back to spread your weight. You should now stop sinking.

3 To get the quicksand to let go, you need to wriggle your stuck parts until they are free.

4 Once you are unstuck, you need to get back to solid ground. If you have a friend, get them to pull you out — but make them do it very slowly at first or they'll pull your arms out of their sockets!

BEAR SAYS

Swamps, bogs, and marshes are even deadlier than quicksand! Stay clear of them. If you do fall in, do not panic or flail around. Call for help. You need to float yourself free.

5 If you are alone, use swimming or snakelike motions. It may take hours to move a few feet, but you can take a rest break at any time.

JUNGLE JUMBOS

Elephants are found in jungles and savannah grasslands of Africa and Asia. They can be fierce and dangerous, but their intelligence and great strength also mean they can be a great help to an explorer.

How to survive an elephant attack

- Keep downwind of elephants and give them lots of space to start with.

- If one starts charging, stand still – running may encourage it.

- If the elephant has its ears out, it's probably a mock charge. Wait until it's stopped and then move slowly away.

- If the elephant's ears are back, it's probably not kidding. Find a large tree and climb it as quickly as possible.

- If there are no trees, throw a decoy, like a hat or backpack. The elephant may start attacking it, giving you time to escape.

- If all else fails, squeeze into a hiding place or curl up into as small a ball as possible.

Ears out – mock attack, stand your ground

Ears back – uh-oh, this elephant is really angry!

TUSK RIDER

When explorer Mike Fay was charged by an elephant in Gabon, Africa, in 2002, he grabbed hold of its tusks and rode them. It was a clever plan, because then the elephant couldn't stab him with them.

How to ride an elephant

You can only ride a tame elephant (try riding a wild one and you will end up dead), and only Indian elephants can be tamed, so if you're in Africa, forget about it.

1 Get on board. Give the elephant the command for "lift" – it should raise its foot to form a natural ladder. Grab hold of an ear and put your foot on the leg, then grab a rope or part of the saddle and pull yourself on.

2 Practice giving the commands for "forward," "left," "right," etc. Use your knees to give nudges behind the ears.

BEAR SAYS

If you are lost in the wild with no water, you can squeeze life-saving fluid from fresh elephant dung. But do NOT touch any other animal's poop because it will make you very sick!

3 Tap the elephant's back. This is the signal for the elephant to sit down so you can get off.

If you're faced with a rushing river, hitching a lift on a tame elephant can be a safe way to cross.

BITE BACK

Most snakes are shy and want to avoid you, but some can be aggressive and may attack without warning.

Snakes to avoid

Fer-de-lance

Tiger snake

King cobra

Brown snake

Tropical rattlesnake

Bushmaster

Black mamba

Coastal taipan

SNAKE SNACK

Many snake species are endangered, but if you have to kill a snake because you are starving, your best bet is to break its back with a heavy stick or club. Aim for just below its head. Use a forked stick to hold its head still and then cut off the head with your machete. But be careful – dead snakes can still bite you!

WHAT TO DO IF YOU ARE BITTEN

If you are bitten by a snake, do not panic. Do not wash the bite, as venom left on the skin could identify the snake. Those are the don'ts. Here's what you should do:

- Remember what bit you – you need to describe the snake so you get the right antivenin.

- Apply a wide pressure bandage over the entire limb.

- Lower the limb – keep the bite below the rest of your body to slow the spread of venom.

- Stay still – if you're with someone, send them to get help, while you stay as motionless as possible. This will help keep your circulation slow and slow down the spread of venom.

- Drink lots of water.

What kind of snake is it?

Send for help.

Drink water.

MIND YOUR STEP!

Snakes can feel vibrations, so one of the best ways to avoid getting bitten is to stomp. But mind where you're stomping! When walking in the jungle or savannah, look at the ground to make sure you're not treading on a snake. When you come to a log, don't step over it without looking on the other side.

BEAR SAYS

In an emergency, grill snake over a campfire. It's sinewy and bony, but full of protein.

BIG GAME

The savannah of Africa is famous for its big, dangerous beasts. Lions and leopards are pretty lethal, but not the most deadly of all. So what is the animal that's polished off the most explorers? Believe it or not, it's the hippo.

Buffalo bash

As a modern explorer, you are more interested in shooting animals with a camera than a gun, but the Cape buffalo doesn't know that. This animal is the ultimate enemy for the big-game hunter – if you bother one, it gets angrier and angrier. Cape buffalo can weigh up to 2,200 pounds, and can run at 35 mph. In Africa, they are nicknamed the "Black Death" because they are so mean.

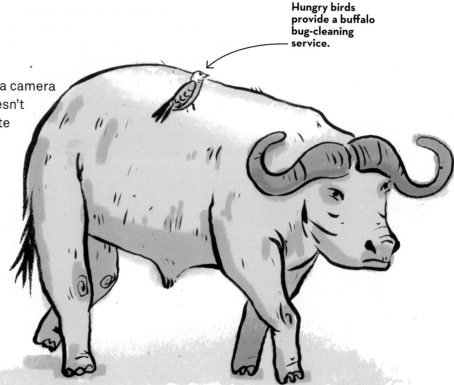

Hungry birds provide a buffalo bug-cleaning service.

Lethal lions

Lions generally don't attack humans, although sometimes they go bad and become terrifying man-eaters (see page 32). If a lion is coming for you and you are stuck in the open, do not run! Stand your ground and wave your arms to make yourself look bigger. Hopefully the lion is only mock charging you, but if it is for real you have two options. You can play dead by lying down on your front, and hope the lion loses interest. Or if the lion is definitely trying to eat you, thrash and yell – it might put the lion off.

Horrible hippos

Hippos are bad-tempered and unpredictable, and have huge chomping teeth. They can run faster than you and climb steep riverbanks, but they are most dangerous in the water. As an explorer you depend on rivers and lakes to get around, but as far as the hippo is concerned this just makes you a target. Hippos like to come up underneath boats, overturn them, and then chomp people. Another charming habit of the hippo is to spray poop out of its bottom while twirling its tail like a propeller, spraying muck in all directions.

The leopard's spots camouflage it so it can move stealthily through the shadows.

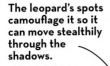

Leaping leopards

Leopards are the least likely of all these animals to attack you – they generally avoid humans. Only if they are wounded or ill are they likely to become dangerous. Keep safe by staying away from leopard cubs, and if a leopard charges you, shout, clap your hands, and wave your arms to deter it.

BEAR SAYS

When I came across a herd of hippos in Kenya, I remembered two important rules. One: never get between a hippo and the water. Two: don't get too close to a hippo's young.

AFRICAN ADVENTURERS

The Nile is the world's longest river, and one of the most mysterious. The hunt for the source of the Nile was one of the great prizes in the history of exploration. Many Europeans set off to Africa to investigate with big plans but little knowledge. Many did not return.

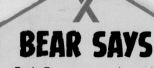

BEAR SAYS

Early European explorers in Africa were brave, but if bravery is not teamed with knowledge, suitable gear, and respect for local people, it's nothing more than a recipe for disaster.

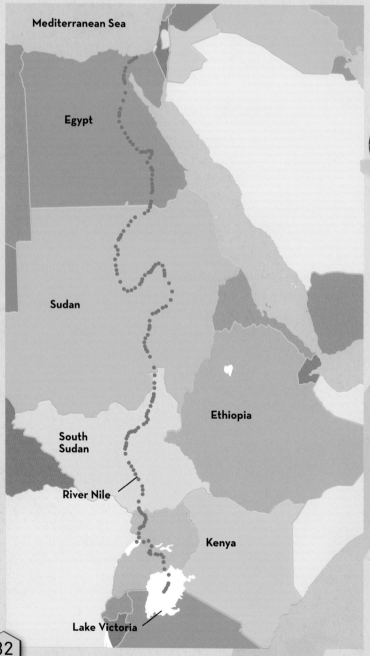

Mediterranean Sea

Egypt

Sudan

South Sudan

River Nile

Ethiopia

Kenya

Lake Victoria

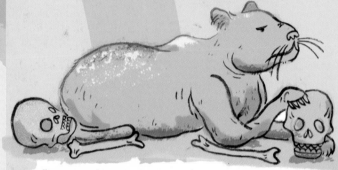

Man-eaters of Tsavo

Colonel John Henry Patterson was a surveyor in charge of a British scheme to build a railway bridge across the Tsavo River in Kenya. The project was stopped in March 1898 when man-eating lions started attacking and killing the railway workers. According to Patterson, two large male lions killed 135 people. Their ability to get through fences and sneak past guards led the terrified workers to call them the "Ghost" and the "Darkness."

Patterson spent months trying to shoot the lions, finally managing to kill the first one in December and the second one a few weeks later. The first lion was almost 10 feet long, and eight men were needed to carry the body. It turned out that at least one of the lions had dental problems, which meant it could not hunt its normal meals and turned to hunting humans instead.

Tragic trek

In 1857 the English explorers Richard Burton and John Hanning Speke set off from the East African coast towards a series of lakes they had heard rumors about. After struggling for months with terrible illness and unfriendly locals, they reached Lake Tanganyika in 1858. Burton was too ill to go much farther, but Speke went north and discovered Lake Victoria, which he believed to be the source of the Nile.

The two men argued about whether the lake really was the Nile's source, so Speke returned there in 1862, trying to prove it once and for all.

Although Speke found the place where the Nile flows out of Lake Victoria, he was not able to follow the river all the way down because of the hostility of local people. (Today, we are still not entirely sure, but we think the Nile probably starts a little farther south than Lake Victoria.)

In 1864, a day before Burton and Speke were supposed to meet in London to discuss their argument, Speke shot himself while out hunting.

Was it a terrible accident, or was Speke so upset about fighting with his former friend that he ended his own life on purpose?

Burton and Speke didn't go exploring alone. This is who and what they took with them:

- 36 African porters

- 30 pack donkeys (with 4 donkey drivers)

- 13 Pakistani soldiers

- 10 slaves to carry the soldiers' guns

- 1 ironclad boat

DESERT

An enormous sand dune as high as a three-story building blocks your way. Soon it will be hot enough to fry an egg on your water bottle, and the sand will start to burn your feet through your boots. Can you uncover the hidden mysteries of the desert, armed with little more than a bad-tempered camel, a plastic bag, and a headscarf soaked with pee?

EXPLORER'S QUEST

The desert sands conceal incredible secrets and undiscovered mysteries, from lost armies of the ancient world to the most extreme animals on Earth. What will you discover?

The lost army of Cambyses

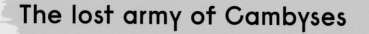

Cambyses was a Persian emperor and conqueror of Egypt. In the year 252 BCE he sent a massive army of 50,000 heavily armed warriors to invade the mysterious oasis kingdom of Siwa, where the great temple of the Egyptian god Amun-Ra was located. The story goes that a huge sandstorm swallowed up the army as they struggled across the desert, and they vanished without a trace – every single one of them. The last resting place of Cambyses' army remains one of history's great mysteries. Located deep within Egypt's forbidding Western Desert, where boiling winds of over 100°F blow for days on end, this warriors' graveyard would be a priceless treasure trove of ancient weapons and other relics, winning fortune and glory for the explorer who discovers its whereabouts. Of course, that's if the story is true...

BEAR SAYS

Study the animals of the desert for a crash course in vital survival skills. They teach us how to find and conserve water, and they show us how to protect ourselves from the burning sun.

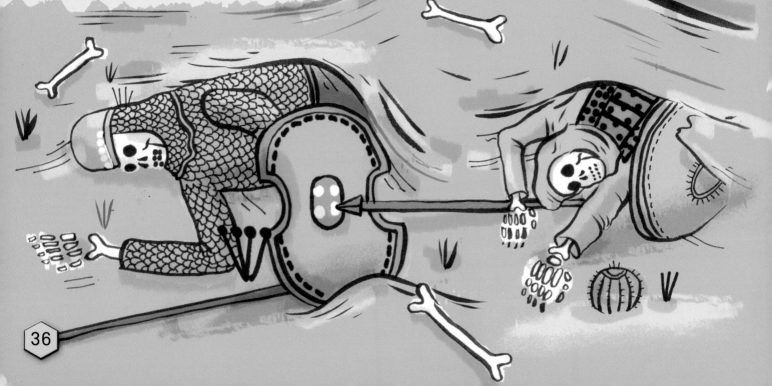

ROCK ART OF THE DEEP DESERT

On a rocky plateau hidden deep within the Sahara is remarkable evidence that the world's most enormous desert was once a lush, watery paradise. Prehistoric rock art shows animals that lived here over 6,500 years ago, including giraffes, crocodiles, and hippos. Once there must have been rivers and lakes here, but now there is only sand and rock. Can you track down these ancient and sacred artworks?

Extreme animals of the desert

In the hellish desert environment, it seems impossible that anything could survive, but there are animals who can take the heat. These special species have unique adaptations that allow them to resist the heat and survive with little water. Can you discover which animal is the ultimate desert survivor?

Kangaroo rat

Tok tokkie beetle

- Camels can lose up to 40 percent of the water from their blood and still survive.

- Kangaroo rats of North America's hottest deserts, such as the Mojave and Sonoran, build air-conditioned burrows and never need to drink.

- Tok tokkie, or fog-basking, beetles stick their bottoms in the air during the frosty desert mornings, so that dew will collect there and run down to their mouths.

UNEXPECTED DESERT

The popular image of a desert is of sand dunes as far as the eye can see, but there is more to deserts than just sand. The deserts of the world include an amazing variety of landscapes and even temperatures – remember, what makes a desert isn't heat, but lack of water.

Rain shadow

Mountain range

Driest desert

The driest place on Earth is the Atacama Desert in South America. There are parts of this desert where it has never rained – at least not since records began. Why is it so dry? The tall mountains that separate the Atacama from the jungles of the Amazon Basin form an impassable barrier for rain clouds. All the rain falls on the mountains, leaving the Atacama Desert in their "rain shadow."

Skyscraper sand dunes

Sand dunes form where the wind piles up sand. If you've only ever seen a dune at the beach, it can be a shock to realize that tiny grains of loose sand can pile up into giant mountains almost 1,000 feet high, as tall as a skyscraper.

The empty quarter

The immense desert known in Arabic as the Rub al Khali ("the quarter of emptiness") is what you think of when you close your eyes and imagine a desert – a vast stretch of sand known as a sand sea. In fact, the Rub al Khali is the largest sand sea on Earth. Crossing this sandy wasteland is seen as the ultimate challenge for the desert explorer.

BEAR SAYS

It is easy to become disoriented among the shifting sand dunes and featureless landscapes of the desert. Practice your navigation skills using a compass and always trust it.

Cold deserts

Deserts like the Gobi Desert of Central Asia get extremely cold because they are high up. In the Gobi it is common to see frost on sand dunes. The coldest desert in the world is actually made of water – in the form of ice! In the middle of Antarctica it never rains and hardly ever snows.

FINDING WATER

You can lose up to four cups of water an hour in the desert. Since deserts by definition are very dry places, you're not likely to find this much water helpfully lying around, so your number-one priority is to preserve water – stay in the shade and try not to do too much unless you have a plan. If your own supplies are running low, you need to find a plentiful source of clean water. If you know where – and how – to look, you can find these even in a desert.

Follow the clues...

Spot green
Although valleys, gullies, and riverbeds may look dry, there will often be water beneath the surface, especially at the outsides of dry river bends and wherever you see green plants growing. Dig a hole and wait for it to fill with water. Empty out the first, dirtiest hole full of water and let it refill. Try lining the hole with stones to keep the water clean.

Track animals
Desert animals will be regular visitors to reliable sources of water, so look out for fresh animal droppings and animal trails (especially ones coming together or all leading in the same direction).

Telltale poo

Tracks to water

Watch birds

Desert birds drink early in the morning or late in the day. If you see some flying past they may be on their way towards water, or if they are flying low they might be on their way back with heavy bellies full of water.

Detect critters

These creatures don't stray far from water. If you see a fly, you are probably within half an hour's walk of water. If you see a mosquito, you must be very close. Ants climbing up a tree may be heading towards a small pool of water that has collected in the branches.

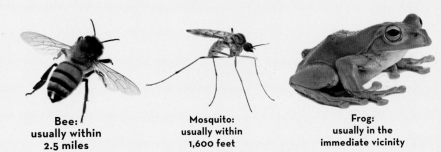

Bee: usually within 2.5 miles

Mosquito: usually within 1,600 feet

Frog: usually in the immediate vicinity

DRINK WITH CARE

Remember that desert water will often be dirty and even poisonous, so you need to filter and purify it. In the desert, a simple method of purifying water is to leave a clear plastic bottle of water in direct sunlight for several hours.

It will take two days to purify the water during very cloudy conditions.

If there's no puddle, start digging!

Find cliffs

When rain falls, some of it will soak into the ground. Some of this water may reappear as a spring, often at the base of a cliff. In very sheltered spots, you may even find puddles left over from the last time it rained.

KNOW YOUR NATURE

Explorers know how to get the most out of nature, and even in the desert there are lots of natural resources. Here's a guide to finding fuel and even a recipe for making drinking water, using plants, a few simple tools, and a sprinkling of knowledge.

Make a solar still

A solar still is a way to use the heat of the sun to get moisture out of the ground. It also gets water out of any plants you can find, and from salty water such as pee. Dig a hole and place a bucket in the middle. Fix a clear plastic sheet over the hole and weight it with a rock so the sheet droops down over the bucket. The sun heats the air under the sheet, evaporating water from the ground and whatever else you put in, which then condenses on the underside of the sheet and drips into the bucket.

Copy the Tuareg of the Sahara

The Tuareg are nomadic people who live in the Sahara. They are known as "the people of the veil," because of the traditional face-covering tagelmust, or headscarf, worn by all men over 25; or as "the blue people," because the indigo dye from the tagelmust stains their skin. Keeping your head and skin covered by loose cotton is a perfect way to stay cool and reduce the amount of water you lose through sweat.

The Tuareg travel across vast areas of desert to find enough food and water. They are brilliant at navigating between oases, and are master camel herders. They use every part of the camel, including its dung, which is vital as fuel for fires because there is very little wood in the desert.

Be careful with that cactus

Everyone thinks that cacti are the drink dispensers of the desert, but cacti are only found in the Americas, and in reality most species are poisonous or too bitter to drink. Exceptions include the fishhook barrel cactus and the cactus fruit known as prickly pear, which you can mash up into a wet pulp.

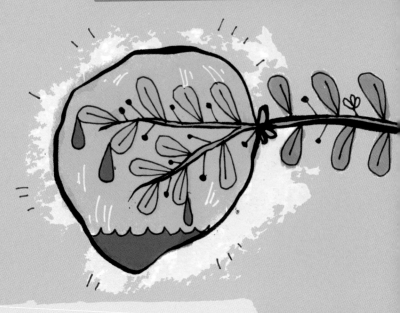

Bag it up

All green plants produce water vapor from their leaves in a process called transpiration. Collect this water by tying a clear plastic bag around a branch or whole plant. Make sure air can't get out but sunlight can get in. After a couple of hours, some water should have collected at the bottom of the bag.

BEAR SAYS

To reduce the amount of water you lose from your body, breathe through your nose rather than your mouth. Travel once the sun has gone down. Try not to waste energy climbing up dunes.

WET, WET, WET

To survive the intense heat of the desert you need to drink up to four times as much water as normal – about four cups an hour during the day, which is equivalent to guzzling three cans of soda every hour for eight hours! The rule of thumb is: if you're sweating, drink. If you're sweating lots, drink lots!

DESERT DANGERS

The desert is beautiful but deadly, and an explorer needs more than a big bottle of water to survive and discover. Danger lurks over every dune, from the stinging scorpion to the mysteries of the mirage.

Sandstorms: death from above

A sandstorm is a cloud of dust and sand picked up by a strong wind, which blows across the desert like a giant scouring pad. Sandstorms can kill by suffocating you, and the fast-moving grains of sand can hurt or blind you. If you see one approaching, take shelter in a building or vehicle if possible. Close all the doors and windows. If there is no shelter, put on goggles and tie a scarf or wet cloth over your face. Try to find a rock to shelter behind, curl up into a ball, and cover your head. Camels simply close their eyes and nostrils and wait out the storm – if you know a friendly camel, get it to "koosh" (see page 47) and use it as a windbreak.

BEAR SAYS

A surprising desert danger is flash floods. When it rains in the desert, it rains hard. Do not pitch camp in a dry riverbed or creek. If there's a storm, it could become a raging torrent.

44

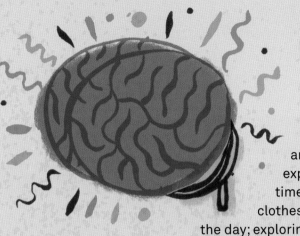

Sunstroke:
the brain boiler

Heatstroke or sunstroke is what happens when your body absorbs heat faster than it can get rid of it. In the fierce sunlight and heat of the desert, sunstroke is the greatest danger facing the explorer. Try to avoid sunstroke by keeping your head covered at all times (see pages 48–49). Wear loose clothing and do not take your clothes off. Stay in the shade, and don't do anything during the heat of the day; exploring is for the early morning, evening, and – if the Moon is full – the nighttime. If you get dizzy or have a headache, stop whatever you are doing and lie down in the shade. Soak your head covering in water and sip water slowly but continuously.

Scorpions:
small but deadly

Related to spiders, scorpions are fearsome looking with their poisonous stinger, but are mostly harmless. However, there are some scorpions that can be deadly, especially to children. How can you tell which ones are dangerous? Look out for small, straw-colored scorpions with long, thin tails – these are the worst. Scorpions generally want to stay away from you, so if you see one give it some room to escape. In the cold desert night, they might crawl into boots, hats, backpacks, or even sleeping bags looking for warmth, so make sure you shake everything out carefully in the morning.

Mirages: tricks of the eye

A mirage is an optical illusion, caused by hot air near the desert surface bending light from the sky. When you see what looks like water in the distance, what you are really seeing is the sky. Don't be fooled!

CAPABLE CAMELS

Camels are amazing creatures: they can go without water for more than ten times longer than you can, and when they fill up they drink up to 40 gallons at once (enough to kill you several times over). A camel is essential for any desert explorer. It can lug your water and tent; provide shade from the sun, shelter from sandstorms, and warmth at night; and carry you places even a 4WD vehicle could never reach.

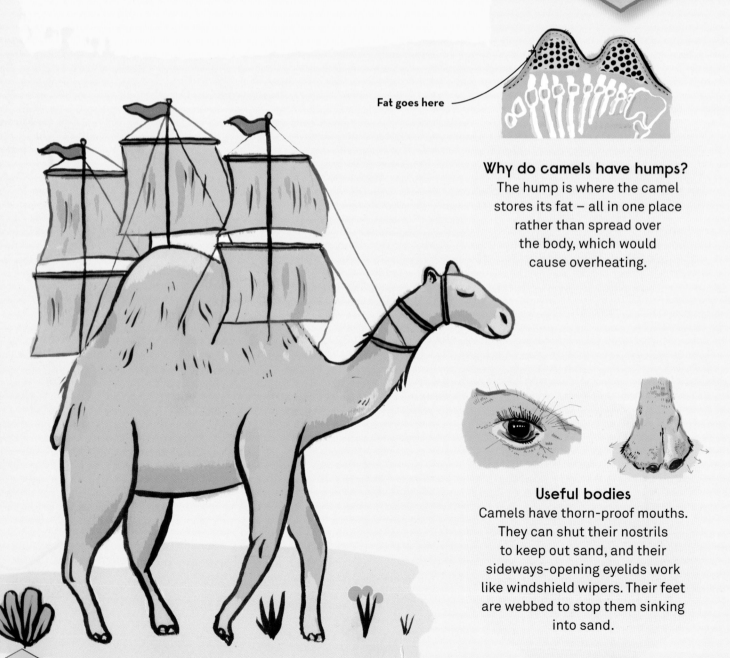

Fat goes here

Why do camels have humps?
The hump is where the camel stores its fat – all in one place rather than spread over the body, which would cause overheating.

Useful bodies
Camels have thorn-proof mouths. They can shut their nostrils to keep out sand, and their sideways-opening eyelids work like windshield wipers. Their feet are webbed to stop them sinking into sand.

Harry the Horrible

Harry was the first ever camel in Australia, brought over from the Canary Islands in 1840. Six years later he was recruited by explorer John Ainsworth Horrocks for an expedition into the Outback, but it didn't work out for either of them. While exploring a dried-up lake, Horrocks stopped to shoot a bird. As Horrocks was loading his gun, Harry lurched sideways and his saddle caught on the trigger. The gun went off, blasting Horrocks in the jaw. The unfortunate explorer died from an infection three weeks later, but got his revenge by giving orders for Harry to be shot! Bad-tempered Harry managed to bite his executioner on the hand before the deed was done.

HOW TO TAME A WILD CAMEL

1 Round up some wild camels and put them together in a fenced yard. Pick your camel with care. A two- to three-year-old female is best. Avoid angry-looking males.

2 Use a "coach" camel to help. Having a coach camel that is already tame and trained will reassure and calm the wild camel.

3 Let your camel get used to you. Eventually she will be comfortable with your presence and touch, especially if you bribe her with food and salt licks.

4 A halter is what you use to guide the camel around and eventually to ride it. Start by getting the camel used to having a rope over and then around her neck. Then train her to move her head and then her whole body in response to pressure on the halter ropes.

5 Koosh train your camel. "Koosh" is the command you give to a camel to make her kneel down so you can get on.

6 It's time to ride your camel! When you get on the kooshing camel, wrap your legs around the saddle horn or hump. Get ready to be tipped at an alarming angle when she gets up on her hind legs and then front legs.

WHERE DID YOU GET THAT HAT?

Dressing up is half the fun of being an explorer! Wearing the right thing on your head will save your life – but what is the right thing? It depends who you want to copy. Do you see yourself as a member of the French Foreign Legion, or would you prefer to be a desert tribesman, like the Tuareg?

BEAR SAYS

Here's a way to stop you overheating if you need to save your valuable drinking water. Pee on a T-shirt and wrap it around your forehead. It will cool you right down. I've done it many times!

Indigo dye is made from soaked and fermented leaves.

Tagelmust

A tagelmust is a scarf that winds around the head and covers the face, so that a single piece of cloth can protect you from the sun and keep out sand and dust. The Tuareg (see page 42) wear a blue tagelmust, while Bedouin often wear a black one. Dark colors screen out harmful sunlight, like sunglasses for your head, but they also soak up the heat more. The best combination is probably a dark cloth covered with a light, white cloth.

SAND DUNES

Desert dunes are created by windblown sand. The shape a dune takes depends on the prevailing wind direction and the amount of sand there is to blow about.

Star: Where winds come from three or more different directions, star dunes form.

Parabolic: The horns of these U-shaped dunes point upwind.

Safari hat

This favorite item of African exploration is made from cork or pith, a spongy plant material that can be pressed into almost any shape. The safari hat lets air through, which helps to keep your head cool.

French kepi

Foreign Legionnaires wear hats called kepis. The brim shades the eyes (and adds a touch of military style), while the high boxy part captures an insulating pocket of air. A cloth down the back shades the neck and ears.

Cap and cloth

If you have to improvise, tuck a cloth into the headband of an ordinary cap to create a DIY kepi. You can even soak the neck cloth in water, so that it cools you as the water evaporates in the desert heat.

Cork hat

In the Australian Outback, thirsty flies try to get into your mouth, nose, and eyes to get a drink. The solution to this problem is the cork hat. The corks swing around as you move to stop the flies from landing.

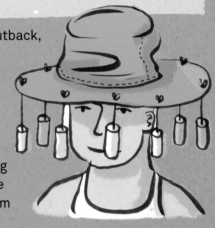

Linear: These dunes form parallel to the average wind direction where sand is plentiful.

Barchan: Crescent-shaped dunes with horns pointing downwind form where wind direction is constant but sand is limited.

DRASTIC MEASURES

The desert is a harsh and potentially dangerous environment.
For safety's sake it's best to travel in a group, tell someone where you are
going, and always get a responsible adult to carry out first aid!
Aron Ralston broke all these rules. When he got stuck in the desert,
he came up with an escape plan – but it was rather a painful one.

Extreme first aid

It's an explorer's worst nightmare. You have
an accident but there's no one around to help.
All of the first-aid procedures described here have
been done at some time by somebody stuck in the
wilderness. While it's important to learn basic first
aid, definitely leave these medical procedures to
someone who knows what they are doing.

Globe luxation

This is the fancy medical term
for when your eyeball pops out
of your head. Happily this will
almost certainly never happen
to you, but it can occur if you
are poked in the eye in exactly
the right (or wrong) way.
To return the eyeball to
its proper place, push gently
on the white bits of the eye
with clean fingers.

Suture

These stitches hold
the sides of a wound
together to help
it heal. They sting
going in and they
sting coming out.

Tooth extraction

Almost nothing hurts as
much as a toothache –
just ask one of the many
explorers who have decided
to tear out a tooth rather
than put up with an aching
one for a minute longer. It
helps to have a pair of pliers
and a strong arm.

Appendectomy

One morning in April 1961 at a remote Antarctic
scientific base, Leonid Rogozov began to feel very
ill. All his symptoms indicated that his appendix had
burst – he had to be operated on or he
would surely die. One problem though:
he was the only doctor at the base
and he would have to operate
on himself!
Fortunately he
had some local
anesthetic available
and some friends
to assist (although
they almost
fainted).

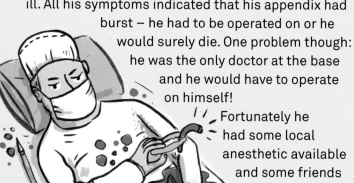

Tracheotomy

A tracheotomy is a
little hole cut in the
throat that allows a
person to breathe when
their airway isn't working.
It can be the only way to
save a person's life if they
have a serious throat injury
or an obstruction that
can't be removed. The hole
needs to be kept open. The
body of a pen or a drinking
straw can help.

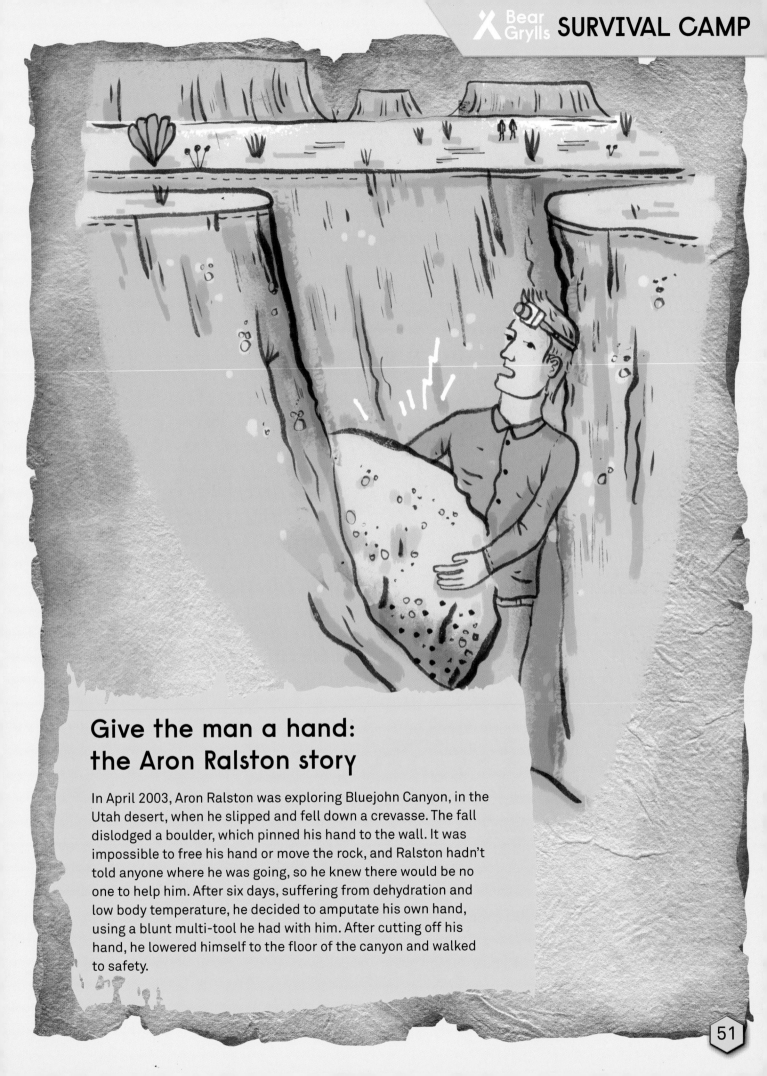

Give the man a hand: the Aron Ralston story

In April 2003, Aron Ralston was exploring Bluejohn Canyon, in the Utah desert, when he slipped and fell down a crevasse. The fall dislodged a boulder, which pinned his hand to the wall. It was impossible to free his hand or move the rock, and Ralston hadn't told anyone where he was going, so he knew there would be no one to help him. After six days, suffering from dehydration and low body temperature, he decided to amputate his own hand, using a blunt multi-tool he had with him. After cutting off his hand, he lowered himself to the floor of the canyon and walked to safety.

POLAR

According to your GPS tracker you are just a two-day hike from the Pole, but things aren't going well. The food for the dogs ran out two days ago; you could butcher one of them to feed to the others, or maybe try producing one of their favorite delicacies – human poop. Now a blizzard is closing in – when the short day ends the temperature will drop to 70 below. Should you press on, turn back, or try to build a shelter using nothing but snow and a shovel?

EXPLORER'S QUEST

The ultimate ends of Earth are the absolute limit of human exploration, and true explorers are always looking to push themselves to the limit. Icy deserts, frozen seas, impenetrable mountains, savage bears, and less savage penguins protect the secrets of the polar regions. What will you discover at the top or bottom of the planet?

Race to the Poles

Unfortunately you've missed your chance to become the first person to reach either the North or South Pole. Although you may be joining this race a little late, the contest to see who can reach the North and South Poles in the most challenging ways possible continues. Perhaps you could be the first person to walk to the South Pole backward, or the first person to kayak to the North Pole if the ice cap keeps melting?

Mountains at the end of the world

The most remote and unexplored mountains on Earth are the Transantarctic Mountains, a range 2,000 miles long and 14,800 feet high that cuts across the polar continent. All the great Antarctic adventurers explored these mountains, but they still hold many secrets – perhaps you could scuba dive in a lake that has been frozen over for millions of years, or look for water in the Dry Valleys, one of the driest environments on Earth?

THE LOST EXPEDITION

In 1845 Sir John Franklin set off into the icy waters of the Canadian Arctic Archipelago to search for the Northwest Passage (see below), but he vanished, along with his two ships and all 127 people aboard. A few bodies and artifacts have been found but the whereabouts of his ships, and most importantly his expedition logs (notes telling the story of the expedition), are still unknown – can you find them?

BEAR SAYS

In 2008, a trip I took to the Antarctic was cut short when I broke my shoulder kite skiing on the ice shelf. High winds meant I had to wait two days to be flown out for medical treatment!

The Northwest Passage

A way for ships to sail from the Atlantic to the Pacific, across the top of North America, was the Holy Grail for Arctic explorers for centuries. In fact there is a sea passage through the islands of the Canadian Arctic Archipelago, but much of it is choked with ice for most of the year. Today less ice forms every year, so there is a greater chance than ever that you could open up a Northwest Passage for the ships of the world.

HOME SWEET DOME

After a hard day's walking or sledding across the ice, you need somewhere to rest and stay warm. And when a polar storm or blizzard arrives, you'd better take shelter or you will soon freeze to death. The Inuit came up with one of the best and simplest ideas – use snow to make a little house that keeps heat inside and won't blow away in the wind: an igloo.

HOW TO BUILD AN IGLOO

1 Mark a circle on the ground, about 6.5 feet across. Stamp down the snow inside the circle until it is hard.

3 Lay the first row of blocks in a circle. Use your saw to cut a ramp in them.

2 Use your saw to cut blocks of hard snow (you may have to dig down to find it). First cut two parallel horizontal lines, then make two vertical cuts.

4 Now lay blocks in a spiral around the ramp. Trim the sides of the blocks so that as you go up they slant inward. The last block should sit in the hole at the top, and should be wider at its top so it is held in place.

BEAR SAYS

You must find shelter before night falls, and with it the temperature. In an emergency, dig a cave in the snow using whatever tools you have. Dig into a slope that faces away from the wind.

Exploring mistakes

Learn from the mistakes of past explorers. When the Duke of Abruzzi went to Alaska in 1897 he took several iron beds with him, as he was too posh to sleep on the floor. In fact, air circulates under a raised bed, so it is warmer to sleep on the floor. Also, remember to bring stuff inside your shelter! When a storm buried his tent in snow, British polar explorer Augustine Courthauld was unable to dig himself out for six weeks because he had left his shovel outside.

5 On the side facing away from the wind, dig down to make an entrance. Use two slabs of hard snow to make a roof for it.

6 A proper igloo has a raised platform around one side, to make a seat and sleeping area.

THE POLAR EXPRESS

Walking on snow and ice in the freezing cold burns up so much energy that you can effectively starve to death in a few days even though you are eating what seem like normal meals. The Inuit long ago learned to use man's best friend to give themselves an easier ride.

Dog driving

Driving a team of dogs while riding a sled is not easy. The traces (the ropes that hold the dogs together and attach them to the sled) get easily tangled, and the dogs fight and may become lazy if not properly commanded. Your sled should have a handlebar, skis or runners, and a brake.

BEAR SAYS

I'm a big dog lover so I am happy to say that today, dogs are not harmed at all when dog-sledding. When I went sledding, I loved working as a team with a barking, rushing pack of furry huskies!

1 Keep your foot hard on the brake until you are ready.

2 Ease off on the brake and give the "go" command (such as "Mush!").

3 Brace yourself for a jerk when you start off.

4 You may need to push with one foot as though you were on a scooter to get the dogs going.

5 Keep some pressure on the brake until the dogs have pulled the lines taut.

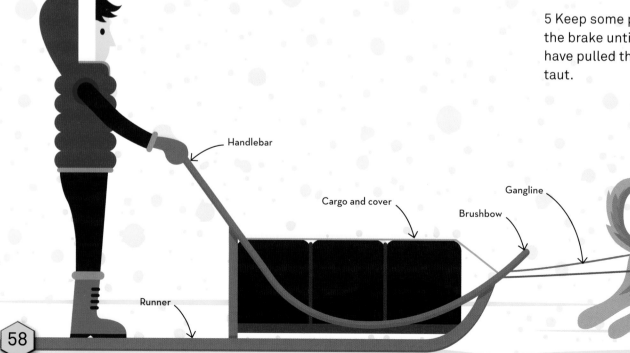

Handlebar

Cargo and cover

Gangline

Brushbow

Runner

DOG'S DINNER

In 1911 Amundsen and Scott raced to reach the South Pole (see pages 62–63). Amundsen beat Scott and made it back alive. One reason was that he used dogs, whereas Scott hated using dog-sleds so traveled on foot. Sled dogs, or huskies, are strong and light, making them perfect for traveling on snow and ice. They eat meat, so you can hunt for their food as you travel instead of having to bring it with you. It's pretty horrible, but Amundsen also shot some of his dogs and fed them to each other, and to his men. Dogs also like to eat human poop!

6 Turn by leaning on one ski or the other (for example, put weight on the left ski to turn left).

7 Use your knees to absorb bumps and shakes, as you would in skiing or mountain biking.

8 Use the brakes when going downhill to make sure you don't overrun the dogs or slip sideways.

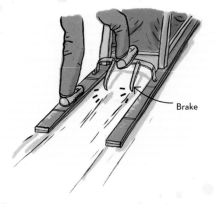

Brake

9 Push with your feet when going uphill, to help the dogs. You may need to run alongside, but don't let go of the handlebars.

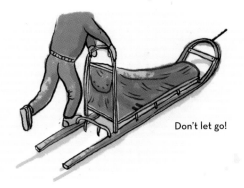

Don't let go!

10 Always watch your dogs to make sure they aren't falling over or getting tangled in the lines.

BEARS AND BITES

Arctic explorers have to worry about two kinds of bites: bear bites and frostbite. At least in the Antarctic there are no bears!

Survive a polar bear attack

Bears are huge and dangerous, but at least most species of bear will avoid you given the chance. Polar bears – the biggest land carnivores on Earth – are different: they will hunt humans, especially if they are hungry.

- If you see a polar bear in the distance, move in the opposite direction. Don't run: back away slowly.

- If one comes toward you, put your hands up in the air and shout and stamp. Sound an air horn if you have one. This will make you seem bigger and scarier, and could make the bear change its mind.

- The best defense against an attacking polar bear is a big gun, but you could try pepper spray.

BEAR SAYS

Only a handful of people have come face-to-face with a polar bear and lived to tell the tale. Set up a trip-wire alarm system around your camp. Take turns to keep watch.

HAMMER TOE

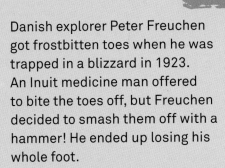

Danish explorer Peter Freuchen got frostbitten toes when he was trapped in a blizzard in 1923. An Inuit medicine man offered to bite the toes off, but Freuchen decided to smash them off with a hammer! He ended up losing his whole foot.

Frostbite

Frostbite is when the blood stops flowing to a part of the body and it freezes. If one of your toes freezes and then thaws out, it won't come back to life: it is dead, and will start rotting. It will also be incredibly painful. The parts of the body most at risk of frostbite are the toes and feet, the fingers and hands, and the nose. If you don't want to lose some or all of these, be careful!

- Keep everything covered with the right sort of gloves and boots: warm and not too tight.

- Watch out for frostnip. This is the first stage of frostbite, which you can recover from: your skin goes pale and loses feeling. It is a warning that you need to take extra care.

- Keep dry. The biggest danger is when your socks or gloves get wet and then freeze. Change your socks often if you need to. Dry out wet socks by putting them inside your underpants (while wearing them!).

- If your feet get badly frostbitten, you are probably better off leaving them frozen. If they thaw out, they will become incredibly painful, but if they stay cold you can still walk on the frozen stumps.

Outer gloves

Inner gloves

Arctic boots

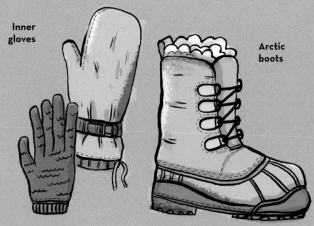

RACE TO THE POLE

The three greatest names in Antarctic exploration are probably Robert Falcon Scott, Ernest Shackleton, and Roald Amundsen. Their successes and disasters offer valuable lessons for trainee explorers.

Shackleton's endurance

In 1914 Ernest Shackleton set out to reach Antarctica, intending to cross from coast to coast, but disaster struck when his ship, the *Endurance*, was trapped in the ice. Eventually the ship was crushed and Shackleton had to lead his crew onto the ice, and then to a small island. The only hope of rescue was to reach the whaling station on South Georgia Island, 800 miles away, in a small lifeboat. Shackleton made it and eventually every one of his men was rescued.

Amundsen the airman

Roald Amundsen was the first to reach the South Pole, in December 1911, and managed to get there and back without losing any men. His success was down to his ruthlessness, careful planning, and attention to detail. Amundsen later became interested in flying, and made the first trans-Arctic flight, but he died in 1928 when his airplane crashed while he was helping search for survivors of an airship disaster. It was probably the only time he hadn't prepared properly.

Bubble burst

The most modern equipment is no good without a decent plan. In 1897 explorer Salomon Andrée set off for the North Pole using all the latest technology, including a hydrogen balloon and remote-controlled oven. But the balloon didn't work properly in the freezing air. Andrée and his crew crashed not far from where they started, and were eaten by bears!

BEAR SAYS

Scott and his team stuck together, right to the bitter end. Teamwork is essential in the wild. It's important that everyone in the team discusses the plan and then commits to it. Together we are stronger.

Scott of the Antarctic

Scott was heroically brave but he made many terrible mistakes. He refused to use sled dogs, and tried instead to use ponies. He and his men mostly hauled their own sleds. His attempt to reach the Pole involved a complicated plan, and he was not as thorough or professional in his preparations as his rival Amundsen. Although Scott made it to the Pole, in January 1912, he was beaten there by Amundsen, and he and his companions died on the way back to base.

FOREST & MOUNTAIN

The mountain peak is hidden by clouds. If you wait for it to clear before trying to reach the summit, the hot sun will set loose a rain of killer boulders and deadly avalanches, but since you spent the night in a bivy sack hanging off a vertical cliff face, above a 900-foot drop to a forest filled with hungry wolves and fierce bears, it would help to see where you are going. On top of all this, you need the bathroom and your zipper is stuck. Should you take off your gloves to fiddle with it, or rub a pencil on the zipper?

EXPLORER'S QUEST

With forests covering their lower slopes and peaks jutting into the sky, mountain ranges attract a very special type of explorer. The type willing to dodge bears and wolves, and brave the terrors of the death zone, to be the first person to stand on top of a mountain. But claiming the first ascent is not the only challenge for explorers in the forest and mountain zone.

Find the Yeti

The people of the Himalayas speak of an apelike beast who lurks among the snowy peaks. Many visiting explorers have seen footprints or claim to have spotted the creature. Can you find proof that the Yeti or Abominable Snowman is real?

BEAR SAYS

In 1998, at age 23, I became one of the youngest Britons to climb Everest. The oldest person to reach the summit was Japanese climber Yuichiro Miura in 2013. He was 80 years old – an incredible man!

Find Mallory and Irvine's camera

George Mallory and Sandy Irvine died in 1924 trying to make the first ascent of Everest (see page 83). No one knows whether they made it to the top before they perished, but the mystery could be solved if Irvine's body is found, and with it the camera he was carrying, which might contain images of the men at the summit. Can you solve the greatest mystery of mountain exploration by tracking down a body lost for nearly a century and recovering an antique camera?

Circumnavigate the taiga belt

The taiga is the immense forest that runs in a belt around the top of the Earth. Pick the right route and you could circumnavigate (travel all the way around) the globe almost without leaving the forest, but would you be able to cope with bears, wolves, and intense cold without losing your way?

Climb an unclimbed monster

Believe it or not, there are lots of mountains in the world that no one has ever climbed. Some of them are almost as high as Mount Everest! You could write your name in the history books by being the first person to get to the top of one of these unclimbed monsters, but you will need to travel somewhere remote.

Track down a living fossil

Hidden away in the mountain ranges of the world are some very special places – isolated valleys where ancient forests still grow. In these unique spots, trees have survived the passing of ice ages, and even the passing of the dinosaurs. Trees like the 80,000-year-old grove of quaking aspens found in Utah, or the Wollemi Pines of Australia's Blue Mountains that until their discovery in 1994 were known only through fossils. Can you penetrate the deep mountains and discover the living remnants of a prehistoric forest?

BIG BAD BEASTS

Since the first humans left Africa and started to move through the endless forests of the north, explorers have battled with terrifying beasts among the trees. Today, there are far fewer big predators of all kinds, including bears and wolves, but if you get lost in the wilderness you still run the risk of becoming food for a hungry animal.

Black bear

Brown bear

Bear necessities

Bears come in different varieties. Polar bears are the most dangerous (see page 60), but in the forest or mountains you could meet brown or black bears. Black bears are smaller and less dangerous. Brown bears, especially the type known as grizzly bears, are big and very dangerous, but even they generally prefer not to attack humans. The greatest danger comes from bumping into one, so that it feels cornered, or from a bear being attracted by the smell of your food. To avoid a bear attack, make a lot of noise as you walk and keep your food "bear safe." Never get between a mother and her cubs. If you see a baby bear, start backing away the way you came.

Front track

Back track

Front track

Back track

BEAR ATTACK!

If you come face to face with a bear...

1 Don't look it in the eye – turn slightly sideways.

2 Do not run! Bears can run faster than you.

3 If the bear is coming for you, stand up straight and wave your hands over your head, yelling and screeching.

4 If the bear still attacks, fall facedown on the ground with your fingers locked around your neck and play dead. If the bear starts biting you, stab it in the eyes or mouth with a knife, or squirt pepper spray in its eyes.

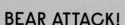

When wolf packs attack

Wolves live and hunt in packs, and they are cunning and dangerous predators. They very rarely attack humans, but if you are alone in a remote place, especially in winter when food is scarce and the wolves are hungry, they may start to hunt you. Here's how to survive a wolf attack:

BEAR SAYS

Wolf packs show us just how formidable a team can be. The pack works together to bring down prey much larger than themselves. Then the wolves take turns to devour the meat.

1 Do not look a wolf in the eye or show your teeth. This looks aggressive and might prompt it to attack.

2 Don't run: the wolf will chase you, and a wolf can run much faster than you.

3 Get on top of a rock or climb a tree if possible.

4 Stand up tall and make yourself look as big as possible. Hold your backpack up or wave your arms above your head.

5 If a wolf attacks, fight back! Aim for the nose. Protect your throat and face with your forearm. If all else fails, ram your hand down its throat – hard.

FRUITS OF THE FOREST

The forest can be frightening, but it is also one of the friendliest places to go exploring, because you can find a fantastic range of things to eat, if you know how and where to look. Explorers like to travel light so living off the land is an essential skill to learn.

Forest feast

What's on the menu? There are 120,000 types of plant in the world that you can eat, and many of them can be found in the forest. Look for the fruits, nuts, seeds, and roots of plants. But beware – there are lots of poisonous plants, so foraging for food is a very dangerous business. Never ever eat anything unless a knowledgeable adult has checked it.

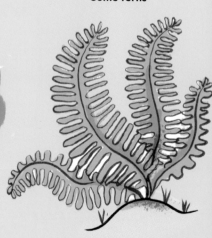

BEAR SAYS

Every year, a handful of people die from eating poisonous mushrooms or berries. The worst offender is the death cap mushroom. It looks like other, harmless mushrooms!

AVOID

- Mushrooms and toadstools unless you are an expert and know which ones are safe.

- Anything from a plant with milky white sap.

- Anything from a red or white plant or a plant covered with fine hairs or spines.

- White or yellow berries. Blue, black, and red berries are often poisonous, too!

Mushrooms and toadstools

Trees with milky sap

POSSIBLY SAFE

- Plants growing in wet soil or in the water.

- Roots, bulbs, and tubers (but always cook them first to destroy any poison).

- Some ferns.

- Blue and black berries, checked by an adult. Berries that have little bits joined together (like a raspberry or blackberry).

- Grass seeds (but don't eat them if there are little black bits growing out of them).

Some ferns

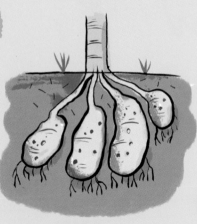

Roots, bulbs, and tubers

Fishy business: DIY fish trap

Mountains and forests are usually wet, which means lots of rivers and streams. Freshwater fish make for terrific eating. A good way to catch them is to make a fish trap. You could make one at home, then try catching a fish in your nearest stream, as long as fishing is allowed there.

1 Cut the top off a large plastic bottle, about two-thirds of the way up.

2 Put some bait in the bottom part – you could use a worm or insect.

3 Turn the top half around and stick it into the bottom half. Make sure the cap is off!

4 When a fish swims through the narrow neck of the bottle to get the bait, it won't be able to find its way out again.

Red or white plants

White berries – or any unknown berry

5 Put the bottle in a stream, at the outside of a bend, in the shade of the overhanging bank. Keep it in place with rocks and sticks.

Plants growing in water

Berries checked by an adult

Grass seeds

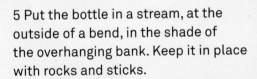

Get knotted

If you are going mountain climbing, you will need plenty of rope, and you will need to practice your knots. Knots are amazingly useful for the explorer. You also need them for everything from building a raft to fixing a rope bridge across a bottomless chasm. Here are three useful knots you can practice at home, but it's worth getting a special book showing you all kinds of different knots!

DOUBLE FISHERMAN'S

Use this knot to tie two ropes together (for instance, when repairing a rope bridge across a gorge).

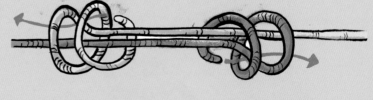

1 Lay the ends of the two ropes together.

2 With each rope, make two turns around both ropes, back in the direction of the rest of the rope.

3 Pass the end through the loops and pull each end tight. You should end up with two "X" shapes.

PRUSIK

A prusik knot slides up and down a rope when unweighted but doesn't slip under a downward force. Use two prusik knots (one for your feet and another clipped to a harness) to ascend a rope.

1 Create a loop of cord. Wrap it around the rope, and back through itself.

2 Repeat this process twice more so there is a triple loop top and bottom.

3 Push the knot together. It will slide up but will hold when pulled downward.

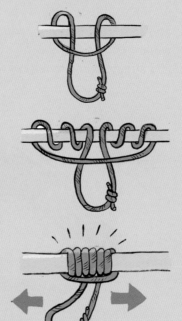

Prusik cord must have a smaller diameter than the main rope.

FIGURE-EIGHT LOOP

This knot provides a good way to make a loop at one end of a rope, which won't get jammed tight.

1 Loop the rope and bend the looped end (called a "bight") around the double "tail." This creates an eye.

2 Push the bight around the tail and up through the eye.

3 Now you have a strong loop you can put over a branch or into a carabiner (a metal clip used by climbers).

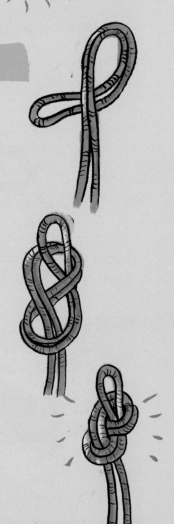

Help from your friends

Climbing is best done with at least two people: one reason why you need a companion is so that you can belay your way up a mountain. Belaying is a method of climbing where there is always one person holding a rope tied to the other person – to catch the climber if he or she falls.

- The first or lead climber goes up first, with a rope tied around her waist, and she fixes "protection" (places where the rope can be fixed to the rock) along the way. If she slips and falls, the second climber, or belayer, is holding the rope taut so the lead climber will only fall as far as the first protection.

- Once the lead climber gets to the top of the slope, she fixes the rope to some protection (such as a rock or tree), and the belayer comes up, picking up the protection as he goes. Then they start all over again for the next pitch.

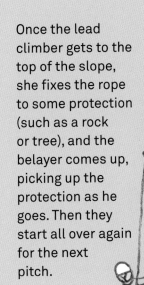

AVALANCHE!

An avalanche is a massive flood of snow traveling at up to 225 mph, pushing hurricane-force winds ahead of it. As a mountain explorer you need to know how to avoid getting hit by an avalanche, and what to do if you can't.

Avalanche danger signs

The most dangerous avalanches are dry snow avalanches where a whole slab of snow slips off the mountainside. These generally travel at around 80 mph, breaking up into chunks and powder as they go. Most people who get killed by an avalanche are walking on the snow slab when it starts sliding, rather than being hit by one from above.

Avalanches are most likely to happen when a lot of snow builds up very quickly on a steep slope. So you need to watch out after a heavy storm or snowfall, and especially where the wind has blown snow onto a slope.

Windblown snow equals danger

Avalanches are more likely to occur on slopes that are being warmed by the sun. In avalanche danger areas, move early in the day or wait until the slopes are in the shade. The other big danger is that your weight will make a slab of snow slip. If you step on snow and cracks go out from your foot, you are in danger. Back away from the slope and look for a better route.

Avoid sunlit slopes

How to survive an avalanche

1 If you see an avalanche coming, try to move out of its way. Shelter behind a rock or tree if possible.

2 If you are caught in the start of an avalanche, try to get to the edge of the slide.

3 Cover your mouth so you don't choke on powder snow.

4 While the avalanche is flowing, it behaves like water. Once it stops, it will start to get hard and solid. If you get caught in one, try to get to the edge using swimming motions, and aim to stay afloat.

5 If you come to a stop underneath the snow, clear a breathing space in front of your face. Do this quickly before the snow sets hard.

6 You will probably be disoriented. Spit or pee to see which way is up – you can tell from the direction the spit or pee is dribbling.

7 You will have to wait for your companions to dig you out. The good news is that the snow is about 70 percent air, but the bad news is that you only have about 20 minutes before the stale air you exhale suffocates you.

ARMED AND DANGEROUS

The 1953 Hunt expedition to Everest was equipped with a mortar (a kind of cannon), so that they could clear away dangerous snow by blasting the slopes with explosives and triggering avalanches. In the end, they only used the mortar as a firework launcher.

BEAR SAYS

I'm not a fan of avalanches at all! I was inches away from death when a colossal avalanche missed me by a whisker in the Himalayas. I just felt grateful that luck was on my side.

THE DEATH ZONE

The mountains are full of dangers for explorers, from mountain sickness to crevasses. Worst of all is the "Death Zone," above 26,000 feet in altitude, where the human body cannot survive without help. Every minute you spend in this zone, your body is dying.

Cracks of doom

A glacier is a frozen river of ice. High mountains often have glaciers filling their valleys, and you might have to cross one. The ice bends and stretches, causing cracks known as crevasses to open up. They can be very narrow but very deep, and what makes them so dangerous is that they can get covered in snow, so you can fall in easily. If you fall into a crevasse, you probably won't ever come out. It is always best to walk around them unless you are part of an experienced team all roped together. That way, if you fall in, your friends can help pull you out again.

Mission impossible

To conquer Everest or other mountains over 26,000 feet, you need to carry oxygen cylinders and breathing equipment, unless you can climb quickly enough to get to the top and back down before you die. The first people to climb Everest without oxygen were Reinhold Messner and Peter Habeler in 1978. Early British explorers thought taking oxygen to help you climb was unsporting, and one of the organizers of the 1922 Everest expedition called anyone who used oxygen a "rotter."

Sick as a dog

Altitude sickness – technically known as acute mountain sickness (AMS) – is what happens when the human body climbs to heights it is not used to. We need oxygen to live, but the higher up you go, the less oxygen there is. In the thin air, you get tired very quickly, you lack energy, you can't think clearly, and you can start seeing and hearing things. You even run the risk of getting a swollen brain, which can easily kill you. To cope with AMS, you need to spend time getting used to high altitudes, moving to higher ground one day at a time.

The best cure for AMS is to head downhill.

79

HOW TO ABSEIL INTO A VOLCANO

A volcano is a crack in Earth's crust, where hot liquid rock (lava), ash, and gas escape from underground. A volcano is an exciting place for an explorer. There aren't many people who've climbed into a volcano (and even fewer who've climbed out!).

BEAR SAYS

Stay away from lava flows, even if they look solid. There can be red-hot lava flowing under a thin surface crust. One mistake can be deadly.

Crazy craters

A typical volcano has a cone made of ash and lava that has cooled into solid rock. At the top of the cone is a crater, which is where most of the lava, ash, and gas come from. Some craters have molten lava at the bottom; others have cracks, with boiling steam and poisonous gas blasting out; and some have cooled enough to become solid and fill up with water, creating a crater lake. Under the lake the pressure could be building, waiting to explode.

Watch where you step!

Beware flying lava bombs.

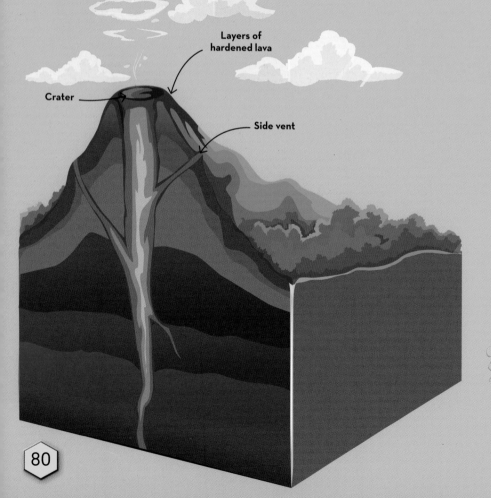

Layers of hardened lava

Crater

Side vent

Gas mask may be required.

THE MOUTH OF HELL

Mount Erebus in Antarctica is a mysterious volcano. The explorer Ernest Shackleton visited in 1908. When he looked into the crater, it was full of steam. In 1955 there was only solid rock in the crater. When New Zealand scientists visited in 1974, it was full of lava. They tried abseiling into the crater to collect molten lava, but the lava lake burped, throwing lava bombs at them. They got out as quickly as they could.

Abseiling basics

1 You can abseil with nothing more than a long piece of rope – it must be at least twice as long as the cliff you want to go down.

2 Loop the rope in half and put the loop over something very strong (e.g. a big rock) – this is your anchor point.

3 Face the anchor point and pass the doubled-up rope between your legs and around the back of your right thigh.

4 Pull the rope up across your chest and over your left shoulder, then back down across your back so you can hold it in front of you with your right hand.

5 Carefully walk backward to the edge of the cliff and lean back. Use your right hand to very slowly release the rope. Make sure you are leaning right out from the slope as you move down.

6 If you are going too fast, bring your right arm around in front of you.

VOLCANO ABSEILING

You will need a harness, rope, a metal descender to control your speed, heat-proof clothes and boots, and oxygen masks. Before descending, test for poisonous gas, and listen to expert advice on whether the volcano is about to blow.

EVEREST EXPLORERS

Everest is a mountain that inspires legends. Two of the greatest are the expeditions of Mallory and Irvine in 1924, and Norgay and Hillary in 1953. The first of them was a heroic failure, resulting in the deaths of both men. The second was a glorious success.

EQUIPMENT: 1953

Clothing

Camera

Oxygen supply

Radio

Tent

EQUIPMENT: TODAY

Clothing

Camera

Satellite phone

Oxygen supply

Tent

Top of the world

The 1953 British expedition to Everest was very well organized and prepared. It had a great leader – John Hunt – who made sure everyone did what they needed to. They had the best equipment, including specially developed boots, tents, and oxygen cylinders, and had scientists working out the best way to use their oxygen. They used clever tricks, like bringing builder's ladders to get across crevasses (a trick still used today). Above all they had teamwork, with some members doing lots of hard climbing and carrying, so that Edmund Hillary and Sherpa Tenzing Norgay had the best possible chance to get to the top.

EVEREST TEAM

Death on Everest

Mallory and Irvine were last seen when some clouds briefly parted. They were two moving specks not far from the summit.

George Mallory was one of the best mountaineers of his time, and Sandy Irvine was an expert in using oxygen cylinders, the new technology that made it possible to climb into the Death Zone. But several things were against the two men. The cylinders available were heavy and leaky, so they may have run out of oxygen. The weather that year was very bad, and Mallory rushed his attempt to reach the top to try to beat snow that was due to arrive. Most importantly, Mallory and Irvine probably chose the wrong route to the top, which is why most experts believe they never made it.

BEAR SAYS

One day you might be on an expedition that starts to go wrong. Perhaps someone will get hurt, a storm will blow up, or you will lose your way. Stop to consider calmly the safest course of action.

ALIVE!

Mountain explorers go into the mountains with lots of equipment and supplies. What happens to people who end up on a mountain without any of these? Could you survive if you were stranded on a mountain?

The miracle of the Andes

In 1972 a Uruguayan plane carrying 45 people crashed in the high Andes Mountains. Some of the passengers died in the crash and others in an avalanche that hit the crashed plane, but 16 of them survived for 72 days. With no other options, the survivors made the difficult decision to eat the only food available – the frozen bodies of their dead friends. Eventually two survivors climbed several mountains and trekked down out of the Andes to get help, using insulation from the airplane they had stitched into a sleeping bag to survive the freezing nights.

DIY SIGNALING FOR RESCUE

If you need rescuing, you should make rescue symbols on the ground so that they can be seen from the air. Try this in your backyard.

- Three of anything is the basic international rescue symbol. For instance, arrange three piles of white stones to form a triangle.

- Use light-colored cloth or white stones, or even branches, to make ground-to-air symbols. "V" means "need help"; an "X" means "need medical help."

- Make the symbols at least 6.5 feet wide and 20 feet high.

Touching the void

In 1985, British climbers Joe Simpson and Simon Yates climbed the West Face of Siula Grande in the Peruvian Andes, a previously unclimbed route. Disaster struck on the way down when Simpson slipped and broke his leg. To get down a cliff, Yates had to lower Simpson on a rope, but Simpson ended up stuck in midair, unable to go up or down. Eventually Yates had to cut the rope. Simpson fell into a deep crevasse in a glacier but survived. He knew that Yates would think he was dead, so he had to ignore the pain, climb up onto the glacier, and hop and crawl back to camp. Without food or water, it took him three days. Somehow, he made it.

OCEANS & RIVERS

Twisting the cloth tight, you squeeze the last drops of water out of the chopped-up fish bones and into your mouth. A frigate bird gets caught in one of your traps. Should you rip out its throat with your teeth and drink its blood, or let it go and follow it to the remote island you are searching for, the one inhabited by a tribe who know the location of buried pirate treasure?

EXPLORER'S QUEST

Exploring the watery world is the closest you can get to exploring outer space without leaving planet Earth. The oceans are completely alien to humans, and even traveling by river can be strange and dangerous. But water is also the explorer's friend – it is easier to travel great distances by boat than on foot, and only by crossing water can you explore truly unknown lands. Which challenge will you go for?

BEAR SAYS

If you decide to kayak down the Amazon River, you'll need to watch out for hungry black caimans and green anacondas, strong currents, and obstacles such as low trees, rocks, and roots.

The mighty Amazon contains more water than any other river in the world.

TREASURE HUNTERS

Treasure hunting is a specialized branch of exploring, combining the excitement of pirates, shipwrecks, and lost gold with the scientific and historical interest of uncovering old coins and ships of bygone eras. There are more than 3 million shipwrecks in the oceans and seas of the world, and some of these contain so much treasure they are worth over a billion dollars each. To give just one example, a Spanish treasure fleet of 11 ships was lost in 1715 off the coast of Florida. Four of the ships, and the fleet's most valuable treasure, the dowry for the Queen of Spain, have never been found. Can you brave storms, strong currents, and sharks to find the priceless jewels of a lost queen?

Fisherman's fiend

There are some very big fish in the sea but you don't expect to be eaten while exploring by river. Meet the Mekong giant catfish and think again. This freshwater monster can be up to 9 feet long and weigh nearly 660 pounds. It is as big as a grizzly bear. Could you catch one while exploring Southeast Asia's mighty Mekong?

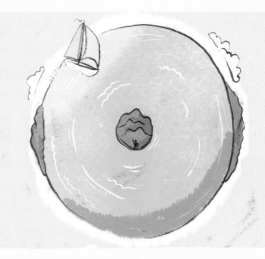

The middle of nowhere

Explorers like to get away from the hustle and bustle, and you can't get any farther away than by visiting one of the world's most remote islands. The speck of land that is officially farthest away from any other speck of land is Bouvet Island in the South Atlantic, 1,090 miles off the coast of Antarctica, and 1,400 miles away from the nearest humans. The most remote inhabited island is Tristan da Cunha, in the South Atlantic about halfway between South Africa and South America. Could you sail there and land safely?

VESSELS OF DISCOVERY

Heading over the horizon without knowing where you are going – or even if there is somewhere to go – is brave, especially when you may have to deal with terrifying storms, giant waves, sea monsters, and scurvy. You need a trustworthy vessel.

Explorers' boats

If you are a billionaire explorer, you might want to equip your luxury super-yacht with a mini submarine, helicopter pad (and helicopter), and a seaplane slingshot launcher. On the other hand, if you are more into classic, solo exploration, you are likely to be interested in one of these three vessels.

1 Yacht

Consider a small sailing yacht with a cozy cabin and equipment that lets you steer and work the sails on your own. This is the sort of boat that single-handed round-the-world sailors use. The modern explorer can take advantage of technology such as satellite tracking systems, so you always know exactly where you are (although this seems like cheating); satellite phones; and sonar and radar to help you avoid obstacles.

TIMELINE OF EXPLORERS' BOATS

Thousands of years ago, the earliest sea explorers were the brave peoples who traveled by canoe to populate places such as Australia and Polynesia. Since those times, sea-going technology has advanced a long way.

Prehistory: Dugout canoe – hollowed-out logs used to paddle close to shore or to reach offshore islands.

400s: Currach – a simple boat made from a wooden frame covered with oak or hides, with a single mast. Irish monks may have reached Iceland as early as CE 790 using these boats.

800s: Outrigger canoe – used by the Polynesians to settle islands spread across thousands of miles of ocean in the Pacific.

800s: Viking longship – a long wooden boat with high pointed ends, equipped with a sail and oars. These had a shallow enough draft to travel rivers but were also capable of crossing oceans.

900s: Junk – Chinese sailing ship. Some versions were enormous, such as the fleet used by 15th-century explorer Admiral Zheng He, who traveled to Africa.

2 Trans-oceanic rowboat

Perhaps you could break the record for the youngest person to row across an ocean? You will need a specialized rowboat, which has an enclosed, waterproof cabin for sleeping and riding out storms, and sliding seats for long hours of rowing.

BEAR SAYS

Anyone can brave the world's oceans in a cruise liner – sometimes the challenge is in the choice of vessel. I've crossed the Atlantic in a small inflatable boat, and rowed the Thames in a bathtub!

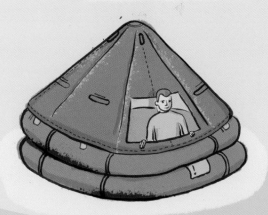

3 Life raft

If things don't go well, you could find yourself adrift in one of these. Modern life rafts have shelters, special pumps for making drinking water out of seawater, and radio beacons to help rescuers find you. But you will still need to know how to survive on the ocean (see pages 94–95).

1450: Caravel – a small but very tough ship with a round belly, high back end, and two lateen (triangular) sails, developed by the Portuguese to explore the coast of Africa and eventually reach Asia and the Americas.

1691: Diving bell – a bell-shaped metal vessel for exploring underwater. The basic technology had existed for 2,000 years, but in 1691 astronomer Edmund Halley designed one for exploring.

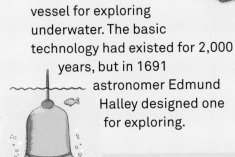

1768: Collier – a ship for carrying coal. The sturdy design of the 18th-century collier made it the perfect ship for Captain Cook's first voyage of exploration. His *Endeavour* explored Australia.

1947: Balsa log raft – explorer Thor Heyerdahl built a raft called the *Kon-Tiki* and sailed it from South America to Polynesia.

1960: Bathyscape – a submersible designed to withstand pressure. The *Trieste* was the first vessel to reach the deepest point on Earth: Challenger Deep.

1968: Bermudan ketch – a small two-masted sailing yacht. Robin Knox-Johnston's ketch *Suhaili* was the first boat to be sailed single-handed nonstop around the world.

2012: Deep-sea submarine – film director James Cameron piloted his specially developed solo submarine *Deepsea Challenger* to the bottom of Challenger Deep, at 35,814 feet below the Pacific Ocean, in 2012.

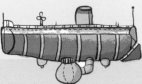

OCEAN DANGERS

Water is not your natural environment – you can't breathe under it, you can't swim as well as any of the creatures that live in it, and in most parts of the world you will lose heat so quickly that you will be dead from the cold within a few hours at most.

Storms

Don't be a fair-weather sailor. Learn how to cope with storms, or you will never sail around Cape Horn at the bottom of South America, or even make it through the Bay of Biscay to exotic France. Watch for storm warnings, such as growing swells (heaving of the ocean) and changes in the color of the sky. Reef (roll up) your sails, so they don't get ripped to shreds by the wind, and put out a sea anchor. This will keep your boat facing the oncoming waves, so you won't capsize.

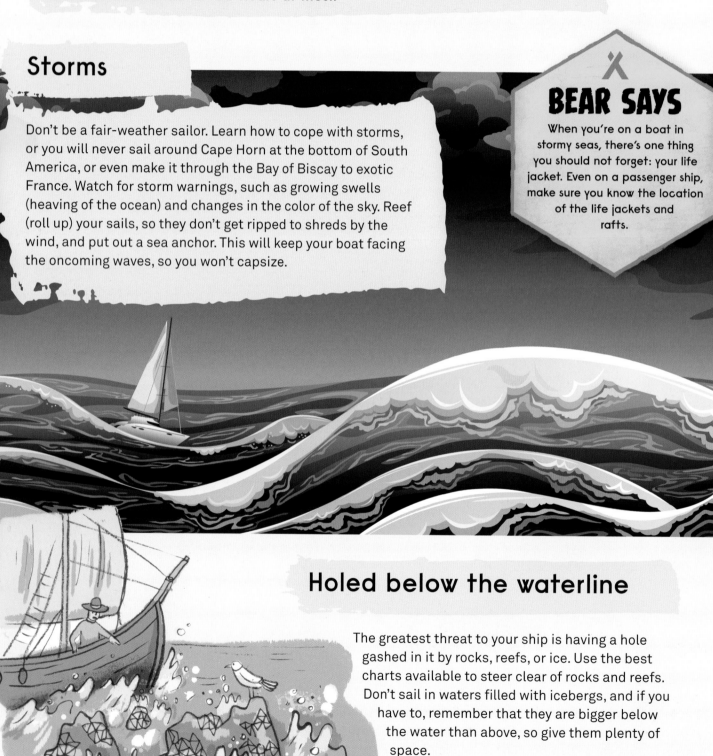

Holed below the waterline

The greatest threat to your ship is having a hole gashed in it by rocks, reefs, or ice. Use the best charts available to steer clear of rocks and reefs. Don't sail in waters filled with icebergs, and if you have to, remember that they are bigger below the water than above, so give them plenty of space.

BATTLE A SHARK

Although sharks are terrifying, you are much more likely to be struck by lightning or fall down a manhole than get eaten by one. However, in shark-infested waters don't go swimming, especially when it gets dark, and don't trail your hands or feet over the edge of the boat. A shark can smell a drop of blood in an Olympic-size swimming pool, so be careful if you have a cut. If you are attacked by a shark, here's what to do.

1 Don't splash about or panic. The shark will think you are a wounded fish and is more likely to attack.

3 If you're with someone else, get back-to-back in the water so it can't sneak up on you. If near a rock or reef, back up against it.

2 Move slowly toward your boat or the shore.

4 If a shark attacks you, fight back! Aim for the eyes and gills, the most sensitive spots, with any weapon you can use or make up. Use a fast stabbing motion.

Expect the unexpected

Danger can come from the most unlikely places. Ask Toby, the pig taken to the Antarctic Ocean in 1904 by French explorer Jean-Baptiste Charcot. Toby ate a bucket of fish without waiting for anyone to take the hooks out of them, and died a painful death.

LOST AT SEA

Disaster! A passing whale has carelessly smashed a hole in your hull. Freezing water crashes into your cabin, waking you to a living nightmare. You have less than a minute to grab what you need and get off your sinking ship!

BEAR SAYS

The hardest decision you will ever make is to abandon ship. But if your vessel is sinking or on fire, you must calmly board your life raft. Once on board, throw out the life ring for other survivors.

Abandon ship

Ocean explorers should always pack a "grab bag" – a large bag containing the essentials for survival. This should include a flashlight, dry clothes, foil blanket, emergency rations, fishing gear, signaling mirror, and flares. In an emergency, activate your inflatable life raft, grab the bag, and go.

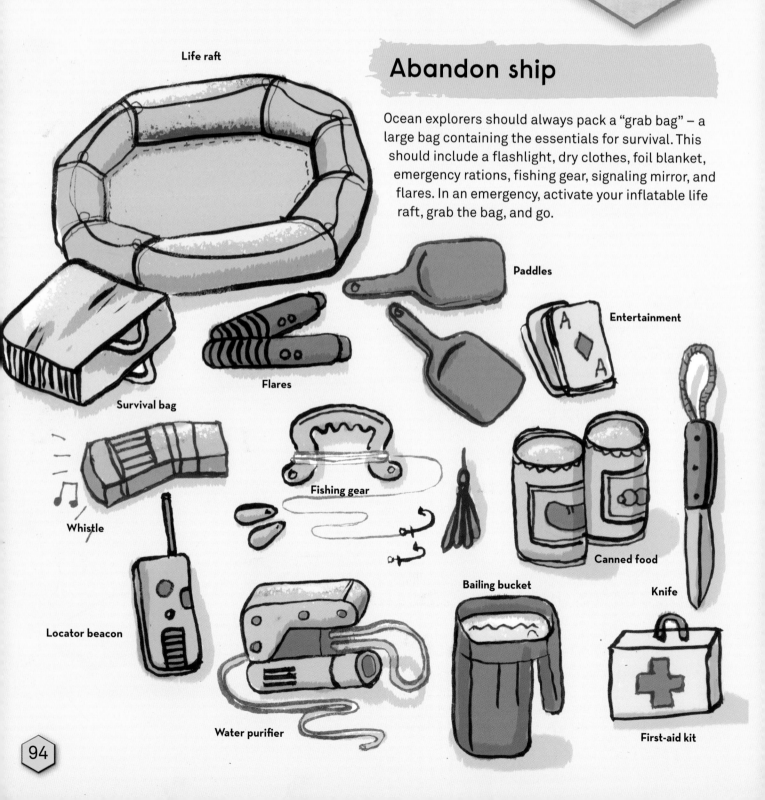

Life raft

Survival bag

Flares

Paddles

Entertainment

Whistle

Fishing gear

Canned food

Knife

Locator beacon

Bailing bucket

Water purifier

First-aid kit

SEA SURVIVAL TIPS

- Never drink seawater. It is too salty and will just make you more thirsty. Eventually it will drive you mad and kill you.

- Don't eat unless you have enough to drink. Digesting food uses up water.

- Don't drink on the first day, so that your body goes into water preservation mode.

- Protect your skin from the sun by smearing oil from fish livers onto it. Dry the livers in the sun first.

- Fish eyes, bones, and flesh are sources of water. Eat the eyes and flesh raw and squeeze the bones in a cloth.

- If you are overheating, soak a cloth in seawater and put it around your neck.

- Water that is not good for drinking can still be used – by putting it up your bottom! This is called a rehydration enema.

DIY compass

To make your compass, you will need a magnet, a needle, a cork, pliers, a thimble, and a bowl of water.

1 Rub the magnet along the needle several times, always in the same direction.

2 Using the pliers and the thimble, push the needle through the middle of the cork, long ways. Warning! This can be difficult and dangerous. Try using a flat piece of cork with a needle-shaped groove across the top, and lay the needle in the groove.

3 Float the cork in a bowl of water on top of a table. The needle should swing around to line up with north and south. You have made your own compass!

BEAR SAYS

Use a mirror, or anything with a shiny surface, to signal for help. Reflect the sun's rays in the direction of a passing ship or plane, flashing the signal on and off. The light can be seen for a long way.

DESERT ISLAND SURVIVAL

Robinson Crusoe is a character from a book by Daniel Defoe: he was shipwrecked on an island and survived. Crusoe was based on a real-life survivor, but don't be fooled into thinking that desert island survival is easy!

BEAR SAYS

When I was a boy, I loved books about adventure and survival. They inspired me to get out into the world and experience all its challenges. I always wanted to be a real-life Robinson Crusoe.

Desert island menu

Your priorities are the same as in any survival situation: find shelter, find water, find food, in that order. On a desert island you need to be careful of sunstroke (see page 45), sunburn, and getting soaked by rain storms. If the island is big enough, there should be streams for fresh water, but otherwise look for coconuts, bamboo, vines, and banana trees, which can all be useful sources of drinking water. Don't eat fish from the reef, as they may be poisonous, but do eat crabs, lobsters, sea urchins, sea cucumbers, mussels, barnacles, and sea slugs. Rinse seaweed in fresh water and then boil it.

Open a coconut

Coconut water is delicious and good for you. If you find a green coconut, cut off the top. A hard brown one is more difficult to break into. Stick a thick branch into the ground and sharpen the end to a point. Use it to split the hairy outer husk and then to make a hole in the top of the shell.

ALEXANDER SELKIRK

Robinson Crusoe was based on real-life Scottish sailor Alexander Selkirk. He was working on a pirate ship in 1704, but he was so sure that the poorly captained ship would sink that he demanded to be abandoned on a tiny uninhabited island called Más a Tierra (now known as Robinson Crusoe Island), 420 miles off the coast of Chile. He sat down and read his Bible, waiting to be rescued, but soon realized that no one was coming. Over four years later, Selkirk was picked up by a passing ship. They discovered a "wild man" dressed in goat skins. Being left behind had saved Selkirk's life because his original ship had indeed sunk and its crew were either drowned or rotting in jail.

Selkirk made friends with some wild cats. They kept rats from attacking him at night.

Message in a bottle

Your best hope of rescue is by building a triangle of signal fires or using a mirror to signal passing aircraft, but you could put a message in a bottle and throw it in the sea. Just don't expect an answer any time soon. Although glass is resistant to seawater, the cork could rot and the bottle could get smashed on rocks. If it catches the right current, it could end up anywhere. One message in a bottle took 92 years (from 1914 to 2006) to travel from the middle of the North Sea to the Shetland Islands – hopefully it wasn't from someone asking to be rescued!

TO BOLDLY GO...

The greatest names in exploration are ocean-going explorers who made incredible voyages of discovery. They were brave men because setting off in a sailing ship across the ocean, when no one knew what was on the other side, was history's equivalent of going into space.

Calamity Columbus

Christopher Columbus is famous as the man who discovered America, although it had already been discovered around 13,000 years ago by prehistoric settlers known today as Native Americans. And the Vikings got there in around CE 1000. And possibly the Polynesians a bit earlier. But Columbus was still a great explorer. An Italian who got backing from the King and Queen of Spain, Columbus thought he could find a new route to Asia by sailing west. Setting off in 1492, he landed on what is now called the Bahamas and went on to explore Cuba and other islands. He returned in three later voyages of discovery. For the Native Americans and Caribbeans, his journeys were disastrous, because he brought disease and death.

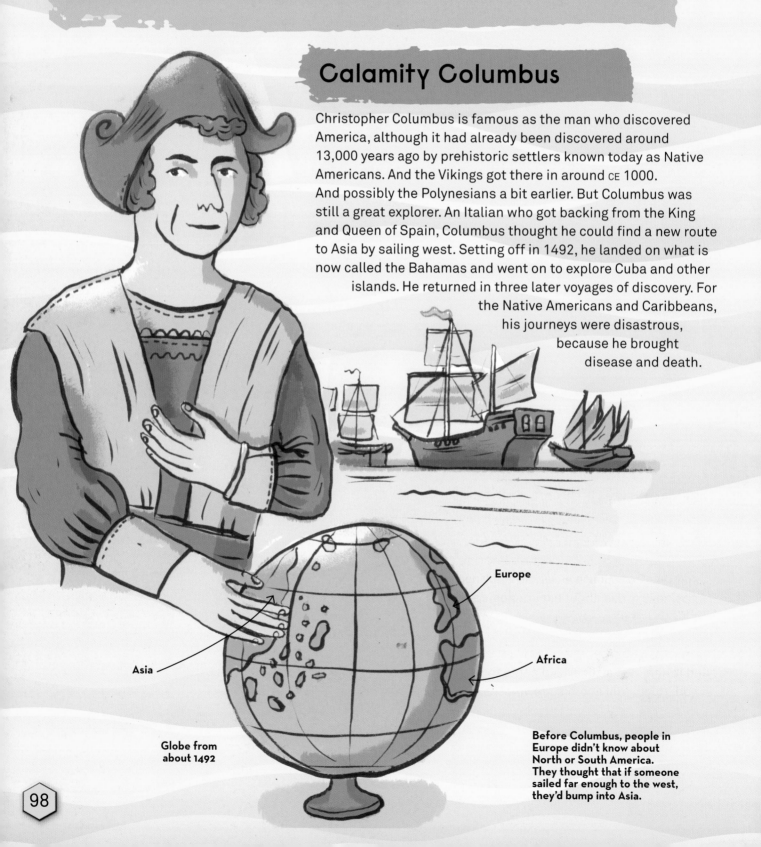

Europe

Asia

Africa

Globe from about 1492

Before Columbus, people in Europe didn't know about North or South America. They thought that if someone sailed far enough to the west, they'd bump into Asia.

A load of junk

Zheng He is possibly the greatest explorer no one has ever heard of. He was prime minister of the Ming dynasty empire of China, and was put in charge of a series of massive expeditions of discovery, trade, and tribute between 1405 and 1433, which traveled through Southeast Asia to India and Africa. He sailed in fleets of junks, Chinese sailing ships. On his fourth voyage he had 63 huge ships, some of which were 260 feet long.

BEAR SAYS

Thor Heyerdahl was told that his plan was foolish and wouldn't work. Don't ever let anyone tell you that your dreams are silly. If you believe in yourself, you will accomplish all your goals.

The Kon-Tiki expedition

In 1947 Norwegian explorer Thor Heyerdahl set out to prove that Polynesia could have been settled by explorers from South America, after hearing Polynesian legends about a mythological god called Tiki who came to Polynesia from the East. In Peru he built a 45-foot-long raft out of nine balsa tree trunks, with a cabin and a mast for sails. He called it *Kon-Tiki*, after an old name for the Inca sun god. Heyerdahl and his crewmates sailed and drifted nearly 4,000 miles until they reached islands near Tahiti.

Balsa wood is very light and strong.

UNDER THE SEA

Technology has made it possible for ocean explorers to go beneath the waves, at first for short periods and only to shallow depths, but now for long periods to the ocean floor. The ocean deeps are the last great frontier for exploration on Earth. It is often said that we know more about the surface of the Moon than the bottom of the sea, yet the oceans cover more than 70 percent of our planet.

GOING DOWN

If you want to explore underwater you have a number of options, depending on how deep you want to go.

Snorkeling

This lets you swim at the surface, looking down while breathing through a tube called a snorkel. Put some fins on your feet and you can move along quite fast.

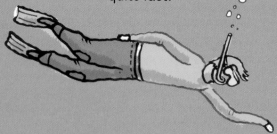

Scuba diving

Scuba (self-contained underwater breathing apparatus) diving uses tanks of compressed air to allow people to breathe underwater. This is the nearest you can get to being a fish.

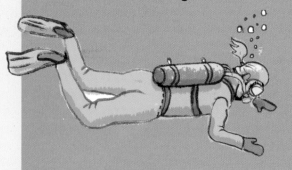

Diving suit

This functions in a similar way to a diving bell – it is basically a diving bell that covers your head, leaving your legs free to walk around on the bottom of the sea.

Submarine

A submarine is a vehicle that travels underwater. The most advanced exploration submarine is *Deepsea Challenger*, which in 2012 descended 6.8 miles to the lowest point on Earth's surface.

Diving bell

If you turn a bucket over in the bathtub and push it down, the air inside is trapped. The water pressure may squash it very slightly but it won't disappear. If you were inside you could breathe the air and look at the bottom of the bathtub. A diving bell works on the same principle. Hoses supply fresh air to replace the air you've used up, and you can look out of the bottom of the bell at the seabed.

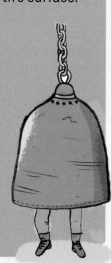

When you free dive your blood gets thicker and your heart slows down.

Under pressure

Free diving is simply swimming underwater while holding your breath. If you know how to equalize the pressure of the air inside your ears with the water pushing into them, there is no limit to how deep you can go, except for how long you can hold your breath. The record is 702 feet, but be warned: free diving is very dangerous. Never, ever dive without an adult dive buddy (someone to keep an eye on you).

BEAR SAYS

Free diving makes you feel like you've entered the world of the fishes. It's a highly dangerous and often deadly sport. The biggest risk is fainting from lack of oxygen to the brain. Always have a buddy nearby.

Greatest sunken treasures of all time

Three of the most valuable sunken treasure shipwrecks of all time are...

- *SS Republic*: A United States Civil War-era steamship loaded with gold and silver that sunk off the coast of Georgia in 1865. It was found in 2003. Salvors have recovered about a quarter of its estimated $300 million worth of coins.

- *Titanic*: The world's most famous shipwreck sank in 1912 after hitting an iceberg in the North Atlantic. Passengers included dozens of the world's richest people, who would have carried their jewels with them, and one treasure hunter believes that $300 million worth of diamonds were on board. The interest in the wreck means anything recovered from it automatically has immense value, but many people argue that salvaging objects from the *Titanic* is grave robbing.

- *Nuestra Señora de Atocha*: The richest wreck ever salvaged, the Atocha was a Spanish treasure galleon that sank off the Florida Keys in 1622. It was carrying treasure from Spanish colonies in the New World to Spain. Treasure hunter Mel Fisher found it in 1985 and over $450 million of treasure has since been recovered.

RIVER DANGERS

What do you think of when you imagine canoeing down a river? Probably clear water running slowly and smoothly between grassy banks, while you paddle lazily along. Wrong! Think again. Rivers can be murky, violent places, hiding deadly dangers that want to kill you (it's probably not personal).

Most-feared fish

Perhaps the most terrifying danger in the world for explorers is the candiru, a tiny catfish with a horrible habit. It lives in the Amazon, where it burrows into the gills of bigger fish and uses its spines to stick there while feeding off their blood. It can squirm into all sorts of narrow passages, including the urethra – that's the tube that you pee out of! Once in there it gets stuck fast and will burrow into your flesh to drink your blood. Explorers should stay covered up while in the Amazon, and keep a safe distance from the water while peeing.

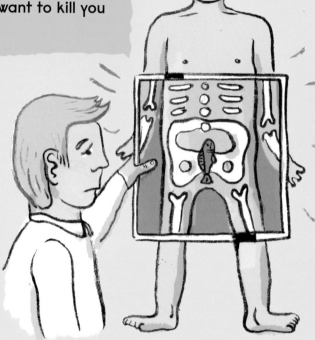

Electric eels

Lurking in muddy pools around the rivers of South America are huge fish with amazing superpowers. Known as electric eels, they are actually relatives of the catfish. They can grow to 8 feet long (about twice the height of an eight-year-old boy). These eels have hundreds of tiny natural batteries in their bodies, and they can give an electric shock five times stronger than you would get from sticking your fingers in an outlet at home – powerful enough to knock a horse off its feet.

BEAR SAYS

As well as being shocking, electric eels are pretty clever – that can be a nasty combination. Watch out for them jumping out of the water to administer shocks with an extra punch.

Bull sharks

This shark species survives happily in the open ocean and hundreds of miles up rivers. Because of their wide distribution and aggression, many experts consider them the most dangerous sharks in the world.

Whirlpools

Whirlpools are circular currents spiraling down into the water. They are formed where streams collide or where the water is blocked by things like big rocks or sharp bends. If the whirlpool is big and strong enough, it can suck down a whole boat – and you with it. This could be deadly news for an open canoe, which will fill with water and sink, but if you're in a kayak you should be fine because most whirlpools die out quickly as they move along the river, allowing you to bob up to the surface. Either way, the best way to handle a whirlpool is to avoid it or, if you can get a good look at it, work out on which side the current is going downstream. Paddle into that part and you can get an acceleration boost that will slingshot you out the other side.

BOATS AND RAFTS

Your boat is not just for carrying you up or down the river – it is also your pack mule, shelter, safety capsule, and, probably, heaviest piece of gear. So you need to make sure you choose the right vessel for your needs. Consider its weight, speed, how easy it is to handle, and how many people it can carry. Hardcore explorers don't believe in cheats like motors or engines, so for a small expedition you have three main choices of self-powered river craft: canoe, kayak, or raft.

Canoe

Based on old Native American boats, canoes are small, narrow, open boats, with seats for two or more people, each using a paddle with a single blade (although you can also use oars, sails, or poles). Canoes are the first choice for most river explorers: good for carrying people and supplies, they can even be carried from one watercourse to another.

BEAR SAYS

A scary moment was when I was floating through jungle rapids after a storm. The water threw me to the edge and pinned me under a rock ledge. Luckily, my camera crew hauled me out!

Kayak

Modeled on old Inuit boats, kayaks look a bit like small canoes, except they usually have covered decks. There are one or two cockpits, depending on how many pilots the kayak has, and each of these is fitted with a spray "skirt" (cover), so that when the pilot is seated there are no gaps to allow water to get into the boat. Kayak pilots use a paddle with a blade at each end. Kayaks are best for explorers who want to go off on their own, or expect to go over rapids, where a river flows over rocks and down steep slopes.

LEWIS AND CLARK'S IRON BOAT

Perhaps the greatest river exploration expedition in history was the Lewis and Clark Expedition of 1804–06. A small party of explorers known as the Corps of Discovery traveled up the Missouri and down the Columbia rivers to reach the Pacific. The Corps used 25 boats of five different types during their epic journey, including an unusual contraption called the Iron Boat. It had a collapsible iron frame so that it could be carried around and set up when needed. Unfortunately, the boat leaked and was abandoned.

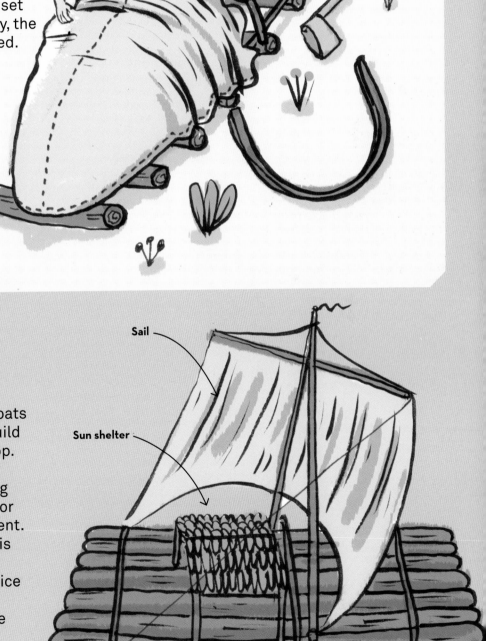

BEAR SAYS

The Iron Boat is a reminder that even the most careful plans can need a rethink!

Raft

A raft is a simple platform that floats on the water, although you can build cabins and other structures on top. Rafts are hard to move and even harder to steer – you can try using sails or poles, but rafts are best for traveling downriver with the current. A raft cannot go over rapids, and is too heavy to pick up and carry, so it is not generally the best choice for an explorer. Even so, some amazing feats of exploration have been carried out by raft, such as the voyage of the *Kon-Tiki* (see page 99). For advice on building your own raft using logs and vines, turn to page 17.

Sail

Sun shelter

ROLLING ON THE RIVER

The river explorer's greatest foes are not crocodiles or piranhas, although these are pretty nasty, but rapids and waterfalls. You could try to canoe or kayak over these, in which case you have to be prepared for your boat to capsize (see opposite); or you could go around them by land, in which case you need to know how to pick up your boat.

Portage

Sometimes you will have to pick up your boat and carry it around an obstacle or to another river on foot – this is called portage. Even though river boats are designed to weigh as little as possible for their size, they are still heavy. In fact, portage can be the most difficult and tiring part of river exploration. Kayaks are light enough to carry like a suitcase or hoist onto your shoulder, but picking up a canoe is a special skill that you will need to practice.

3 Move your forward hand along the yoke bar to grip the far gunwale. Move your other hand along the bar until it reaches the near gunwale. Keep the canoe balanced on your thighs.

1 Face the canoe and grab the near gunwale (rim) in the middle. Lift the side of the canoe and take a step forward.

4 Roll and swing the canoe onto your head.

2 Lean into the canoe and grab the bar across the middle – this is called the carrying yoke. Keep your back straight and lean backward, bending your knees so the canoe lifts onto your thighs.

5 Lower the canoe onto your shoulders so that the yoke bar sits across them. You are now ready to portage your canoe.

Screw roll

Before you set off exploring in your kayak, make sure you know how to roll out of a capsize. One technique is the screw roll.

1 If you roll over, wait until you're upside down, then twist your body, lean forward, reach up, and put your paddle out of the water.

4 When the paddle is pointing straight down, snap up your right hip.

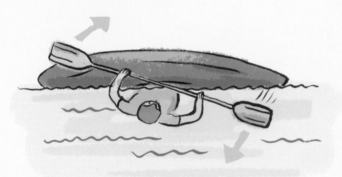

2 Roll your right wrist to make sure the right paddle blade is facing the water. Bring it down into the water in a sweep away from the front of the kayak toward the back.

5 Keep your head and body in the water until the last moment. When the boat rolls level they will come out of the water.

BEAR SAYS

If all else fails and you are still underwater, release your spray skirt, put your hands on the rim of the cockpit, and push the kayak up and forward to get your legs clear so you can float free.

3 The kayak will start to twist. Untwist your body so that you face forward, while still sweeping the paddle back.

GETTING WET FEET

Many great explorers traveled by river for some or all of their voyages of exploration. Rivers are brilliant ways to cover large distances while carrying plenty of equipment and food, but most importantly they will almost always lead you to safety, because if you follow them downstream far enough you will eventually find other people.

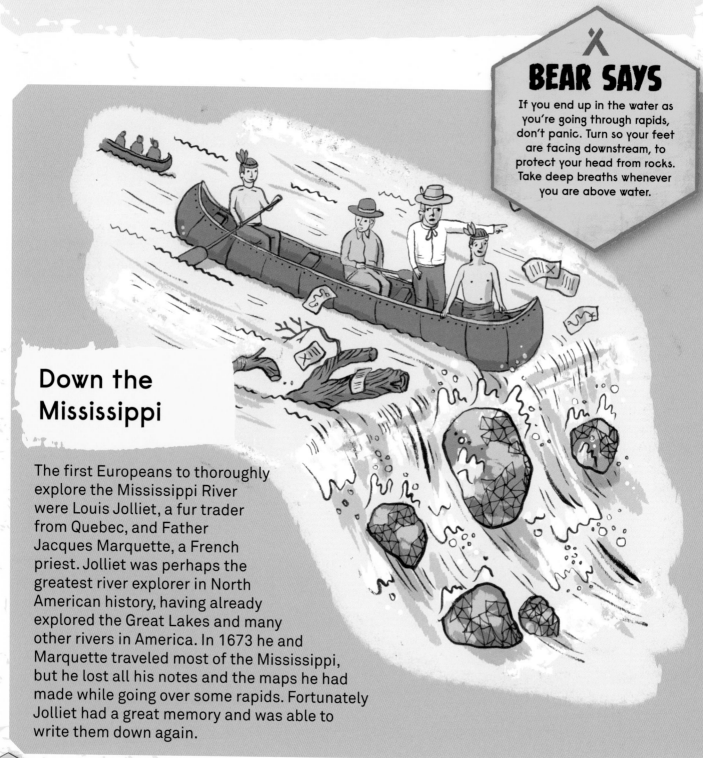

BEAR SAYS

If you end up in the water as you're going through rapids, don't panic. Turn so your feet are facing downstream, to protect your head from rocks. Take deep breaths whenever you are above water.

Down the Mississippi

The first Europeans to thoroughly explore the Mississippi River were Louis Jolliet, a fur trader from Quebec, and Father Jacques Marquette, a French priest. Jolliet was perhaps the greatest river explorer in North American history, having already explored the Great Lakes and many other rivers in America. In 1673 he and Marquette traveled most of the Mississippi, but he lost all his notes and the maps he had made while going over some rapids. Fortunately Jolliet had a great memory and was able to write them down again.

The Amazon by accident

One of the great voyages of river exploration was made by accident in 1538. Spaniard Francisco de Orellana was part of an expedition looking for El Dorado, the fabled city of gold in South America (see page 20). He and his men became separated from the rest of the expedition and decided to build some boats, as he was sure that El Dorado was just around the bend. Eventually he followed the river all the way to the sea, traveling almost the entire length of the Amazon River. He returned to South America in 1546, but the expedition was a disaster and he died.

Maddening mosquitoes

Mina Hubbard's husband, Leonidas, died while exploring the rivers of Labrador, eastern Canada, in 1903. She decided to finish what he had started, so in 1905 she set off down the North West River with the help of four guides. Although they braved fierce rapids, Hubbard's biggest problems were the swarms of mosquitoes and flies that constantly tried to eat her. She wore homemade masks with netting covering her face, but she could feel the blood running down her neck from all the bites! •

DIY DRY BAG

You need a dry bag to hold valuable things so they don't get wet. Use a plastic bag with no holes (e.g. a large freezer bag).

1 Put your stuff (e.g. maps, pictures) inside the bag and squeeze out the air.

2 Roll up the top, from one side to the other.

3 Twist the rolled-up section.

4 Fold it over and put a tight rubber band around the fold.

5 Test it out by putting it underwater in a sink or bathtub.

NAVIGATION

It's dark and you are lost. If only you hadn't shredded your map when you were trying to fold it, and then lost your compass crossing that river! Luckily it's a clear night, with a crescent moon and a good view of the stars – you should have no trouble working out which way is north. The only question is, should you head off in the dark, or wait until morning and find a hill so you can get a good look around you?

MAP READING

Exploring isn't just about having adventures, fighting off sharks, and abseiling into volcanoes (although these are the best bits). Explorers like to visit places where few, if any, people have ever been, but to get there they need to be able to navigate (find their way) using a map, compass, and – sometimes – the Sun, Moon, and stars.

The joy of maps

In the old days the explorer started off with a big blank sheet of paper decorated with some drawings of sea monsters, and it was his or her job to fill it in and make a map. Today there aren't many blank spots left on the map, and as a result, your map is probably your most valuable piece of equipment (after your comfortable walking boots). Before you head off into the wilderness, make sure you know how to use your map. You need to know how to read and fold your map, and how to use it with a compass.

A person who makes maps is called a cartographer.

BEAR SAYS

Never depend on your GPS alone. Make sure your map-reading skills are first class. That way, when your GPS is on the blink, you won't find yourself heading the wrong way off a cliff.

DIY MAP

A map doesn't have to be covered in contours and symbols, but it should show where things are compared to each other. Explorers should be good at making maps, so practice by drawing a map of your house and yard, or maybe your street and neighborhood. Start off by drawing a grid, and try to keep the same scale throughout the map.

Folding a map

This sounds like a simple task but actually it's all too easy to get wrong. Maps are usually big, with lots of folds, so if you do mess it up you will end up with a big bundle of paper that won't fit in your map case, and the map will tear at the folds and fall apart.

1 Open up your map until it is fully spread open.

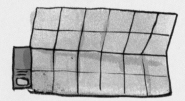

2 Check the creases and folds. If they are fresh, they will indicate where to fold.

3 Fold the map in half, so that the cover is still sticking out of the side.

4 Squeeze the map together like an accordion, but make sure the cover stays on top.

5 Fold over the cover so that it is on the outside.

Walk the line

If you look at your map you will notice two sorts of lines (not counting roads, rivers, railways, etc.). The straight lines that form a grid on your map are lines of longitude and latitude. These are imaginary lines that mapmakers and explorers use as reference points when describing where they are. Lines of longitude run from Pole to Pole. They show where you are from east to west. Lines of latitude circle around Earth parallel to the equator. They show where you are from north to south.

Lines of longitude

Lines of latitude

The other sort of lines on your map are contour lines. A contour line joins up places that are the same height, and they are used to represent hills, mountains, cliffs, and valleys on a flat piece of paper. Contour lines close together mean a steep hill while ones that are spread apart indicate a gentle slope. This is important when planning your route.

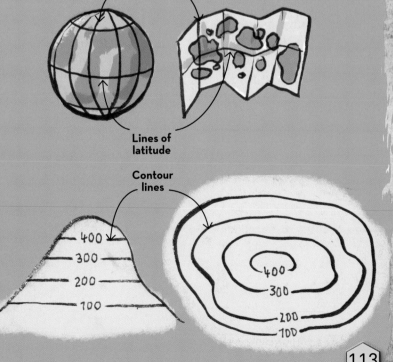

Contour lines

TRUE NORTH

North doesn't just mean "up" on your map. If you understand what north and south mean, and how to find them, you will never get truly lost.

Earth is a giant magnet

Earth is a sphere or globe, and when we say "north" what we really mean is the top of this globe. Earth spins around, and if you imagine it is spinning around a very big stick running through the planet from top to bottom, the North Pole is where the stick comes out of the top of the planet, and the South Pole is where it comes out of the bottom. These places are known as "true north" and "true south." Earth doesn't really have a big stick, but it does have liquid iron in the middle (like a soft-boiled egg with a runny yolk). This iron core makes Earth into a giant magnet.

A compass works because the ends of a metal needle are attracted to the north and south magnetic poles of Earth, so that the compass needle will point to magnetic north.

But Earth's magnetic poles don't line up exactly with "true" north and south. In most of the world you have to make adjustments because of this. If you're exploring near the Poles your compass may not be much use, and you'll have to use a different way of working out north and south.

BEAR SAYS

The key to map reading is to be able to relate what you see on the map to what you see around you. And the reverse. Rely on more than one indicator to confirm where you are.

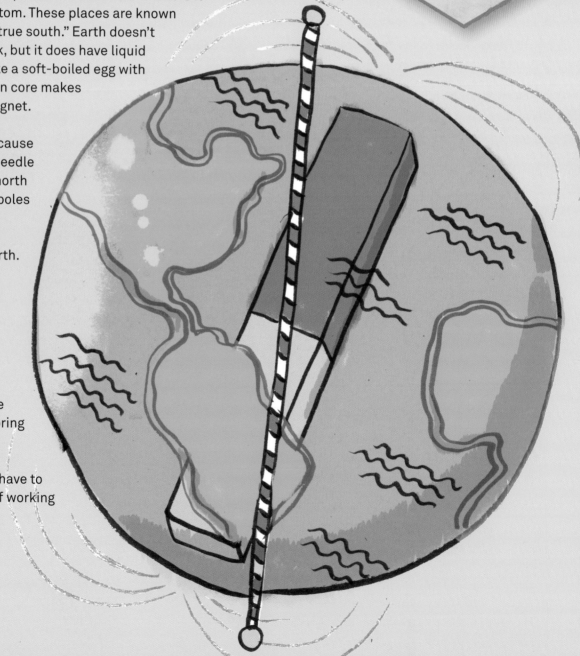

Finding north

There are lots of ways you can find north without a compass – probably the simplest use the movement of the Sun and Moon across the sky. Try out these methods in your backyard.

I Using a watch If you have a wristwatch with hands, put the watch in the palm of your hand and point the hour (little) hand at the Sun. A line pointing halfway between the 12 o'clock marker and the hour hand points south. Before noon, you'll have to measure clockwise from your hour hand to the 12 o'clock marker. In the afternoon, measure counterclockwise. If you are in the southern hemisphere, point the 12 o'clock marker at the Sun and the line between it and the hour hand will be pointing north. If you have a digital watch, draw a clock face on the ground.

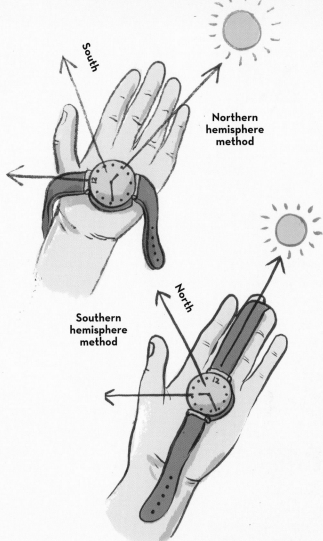

South

Northern hemisphere method

North

Southern hemisphere method

First mark

Second mark

2 Sun stick Put a straight stick upright in the ground in a flat place. Mark the tip of its shadow with a rock. Wait 15 minutes and then mark the shadow's tip again. Stand with your left foot at the first marker and your right foot at the second marker. In the northern hemisphere, you are now facing north. You can do the same thing at night if the Moon is bright enough.

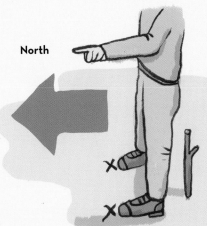

North

COMPASS CLASS

A compass has a needle that points toward the magnetic north pole. Compasses come in many different shapes and sizes, from tiny button ones (keep one of these in your emergency pack) to complicated electronic ones. The most common one for explorers is an orienteering compass.

Natural north

Because the Sun shines from the south, if you are in the northern hemisphere, you can tell which way is north by looking carefully at the trees. In the southern hemisphere, reverse all these signs, because the Sun shines from the north.

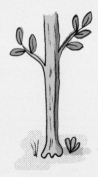   

- Young trees will be lighter on the south side and darker on the north side.

- Branches grow out sideways to the south, but to the north, they stick up.

- A tree on its own will usually have more moss on the north (shady) side.

- Trees growing on a south-facing slope will be thicker and taller.

COMPASS TYPES

 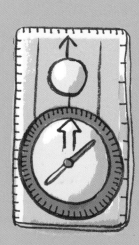 

Ancient Chinese   **Orienteering**   **Mirrored sighting**

Orienteering with a compass

An orienteering compass is made to use with a map. It is fixed into a see-through plastic card with lines on it, and has a dial you can turn, with an arrow. You can use these to make sure your map is the right way around, to decide which direction to go in and to make sure you keep going in the right direction.

To orient your map (i.e. make sure it is lined up with north), follow these steps:

BEAR SAYS

Using your compass and the grid lines on a map, practice giving an exact grid reference for where you are. This is essential for naming a meeting point – or if you need rescue. Horizontals first then verticals!

1 Line up the sides of the compass with the north–south lines on your map.

2 Turn the big arrow until it is pointing to map north.

3 Hold the map and compass together as you turn around, until the red end of the compass needle lines up with the big arrow.

4 Your map is now oriented, and if you draw a line from your position on the map to a landmark (e.g. the top of a hill), you should find that this line points to the landmark in real life.

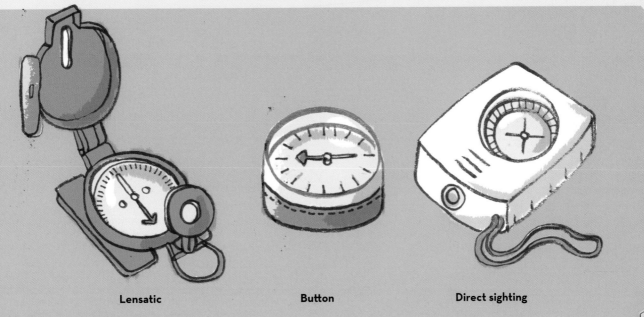

Lensatic   Button   Direct sighting

NAVIGATING BY THE STARS

Try not to get lost in the Antarctic mountains in winter: not only will it be cold enough to kill you in seconds with raging winds that knock you off your feet, but it will be hard to navigate back to base. The Sun never rises and your compass will go haywire because you are too near the southern magnetic pole. Your only hope is to use the stars – the same navigational tools that people have been using since earliest prehistoric times.

BEAR SAYS

If darkness falls as you are trudging the last miles to camp, knowing how to navigate by the stars could save your life! Don't get spooked by the dark – keep your nerve.

Sextant

You can use a sextant to measure the angle between a star (including our nearest star – the Sun) and the horizon. With this information you can calculate your latitude – your position north or south of the Equator. Navy navigators are still taught how to use the sextant in case their electronic systems get blown up in battle.

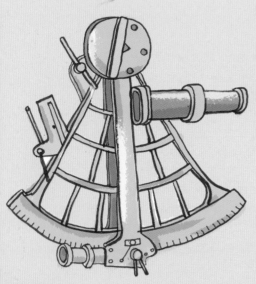

Star movement at the North Pole

Star movement at the Equator

Star movement in between

The sky at night

Look up on a cloudless night and you will see thousands of stars scattered across the sky. With just your eyes you can see around 2,000 stars at a time (if you have binoculars you can see around 50,000). These stars seem to move very slowly across the night sky, but in fact they are not moving – you are, or at least Earth is moving and taking you with it. As Earth rotates toward the east, the stars above seem to move from east to west, like the Sun and Moon. You can use this simple fact to work out north, south, east, and west.

Star tracking

Stars move very slowly so working out which way a star is moving just by looking at it is impossible. You need to watch the star against something close to hand. You can use two sticks stuck in the ground close together and upright, and track how a star moves between them. If you are in the northern hemisphere and the star moves left, it is to the north, if it moves right it is to the south, if it moves up the star is in the east, down and it is in the west.

Star shadow

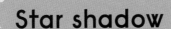

Another method is to hang a string from a stick set in the ground at an angle. Lie on your back with the string by your eye and line it up with a star. Mark the point where the string touches the ground. Follow the star for ten minutes and then do it again. This is the same as the Sun stick method, with the string in place of the shadow the first mark is in the west and the second is in the east.

FINDING NORTH AND SOUTH BY THE STARS

The North or Pole Star, Polaris, is above the North Pole, so all the other stars seem to rotate around it. If you can find it you know which way is north. There is no bright star above the South Pole, but you can find south with the help of the constellation called the Southern Cross.

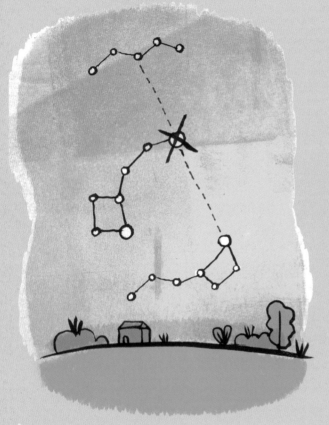

Find the Southern celestial pole

- Find the Milky Way (a milky band across the sky).

- Follow it until you find a dark patch called the Coal Sack.

- Look for a cross of four stars, two of which are very bright. This is the Southern Cross.

- Near the Southern Cross are two bright stars – the pointer stars (Rigil Kent and Hadar). Draw an imaginary line between these stars. The point where this line intersects with a line extended from the long axis of the Southern Cross is the celestial south pole.

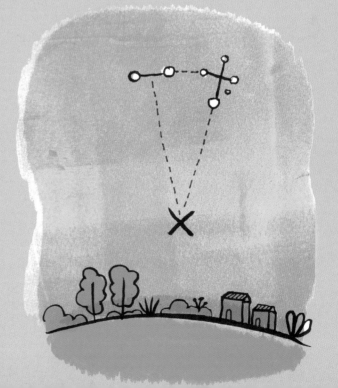

Find the North Star

- Find the Plow (also known as the Big Dipper or Ursa Major). The two stars in the outer edge of the "saucepan" point at the North Star, which is one of the brightest stars in the sky.

- Find Cassiopeia, a constellation that looks like a big "M" or "W." A line pointing straight through the inner angle of the "W" points to the North Star.

- The North Star is the last star in the "handle" of the Little Dipper, also known as Ursa Minor.

By the horns of the Moon!

The Moon goes around Earth once every 28 days. We can only see it when the Sun shines on the side that is facing us. When the Sun shines on the whole of the facing side, we see a full Moon, and when it shines entirely on the opposite side, we can't see the Moon at all (this is called a "new Moon"). In between, the Sun only lights up part of the Moon, so that we see a "crescent Moon."

You can use the crescent Moon as a quick way to find north or south, depending on your hemisphere. The tips of the crescent are known as the "horns." Imagine a straight line between the horns, extending down to the horizon. In the northern hemisphere this line points roughly south, and in the southern hemisphere it points roughly north.

Sastrugi signs

If you are exploring in Antarctica, you don't want to get off course because the landscape is featureless, so there are few landmarks to help you get back on track. A good tip is to use the sastrugi – wavy ridges in the snow, like sand dunes, formed by the wind, which run for great distances in parallel lines. Are you heading straight across them, along them, or at an angle to them? Memorize this information and use it to set your course.

BEAR SAYS

If you get lost, then head down-hill until you find a stream. Follow the stream until it becomes a river and then follow this until you find people.

INDEX

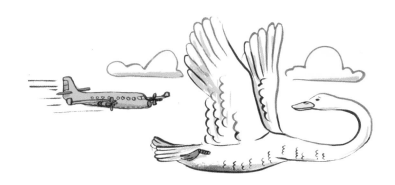

Bear Grylls
SURVIVAL CAMP
The Ultimate All-terrain Training Manual

First American Edition 2017
Kane Miller, A Division of EDC Publishing

Conceived by Weldon Owen in partnership with Bear Grylls Ventures
Produced by Weldon Owen, Suite 3.08 The Plaza, 535 King's Road, London
SW10 0SZ, UK

For information contact:
Kane Miller, A Division of EDC Publishing
PO Box 470663
Tulsa, OK 74147-0663
www.kanemiller.com
www.edcpub.com
www.usbornebooksandmore.com

Library of Congress Control Number: 2017945578

Printed in Malaysia
2 3 4 5 6 7 8 9 10

ISBN: 978-1-61067-755-4

KIDS – if you want to try any of the activities in this book, please ask your
parents first! Parents – all outdoor activities carry some degree of risk and we
recommend that anyone participating in these activities be aware of the risks
involved and seek professional instruction and guidance. None of the health/
medical information in this book is intended as a substitute for professional
medical advice; always seek the advice of a qualified practitioner.

DISCLAIMER
Weldon Owen and Bear Grylls take pride in doing their best to get the
facts right in putting together the information in this book, but occasionally
something slips past their beady eyes. Therefore we make no warranties
about the accuracy or completeness of the information in the book and to the
maximum extent permitted, we disclaim all liability. Wherever possible, we will
endeavor to correct any errors of fact at reprint.

PICTURE CREDITS
While every effort has been made to credit all contributors, Weldon
Owen would like to apologize should there have been any omissions or
errors, and would be pleased to make any appropriate corrections for
future editions of this book.

ILLUSTRATIONS
All illustrations by James Gulliver Hancock/The Jacky Winter Group. All
illustrations copyright Weldon Owen

Discover more amazing books in the Bear Grylls series:

Bear Grylls Extreme Planet
Survival Skills Handbook (Volume 1)

Polar Worlds Activity Book
Wild Survival Activity Book
Animal Detective Activity Book
Dangerous Animals Activity Book
In the Jungle Coloring Book
Reptiles and Amphibians Coloring Book

Bear Grylls Adventures: The Desert Challenge
Bear Grylls Adventures: The Blizzard Challenge
Bear Grylls Adventures: The Jungle Challenge
Bear Grylls Adventures: The Sea Challenge